3/28/94
NORTH CAROLINA
SUGAR MOUNTAIN

Successful Telemarketing
Opportunities and Techniques for Increasing Sales and Profits

Sell as Good for 10⁵⁰

Successful Telemarketing

Opportunities and Techniques for Increasing Sales and Profits

Bob Stone

Chairman Emeritus, Stone & Adler, Inc.
a Young & Rubicam company

John Wyman

Vice President, AT&T

NTC Business Books
NTC a division of *NTC Publishing Group* • Lincolnwood, Illinois USA

1989 Printing

Published by NTC Business Books,
a division of NTC Publishing Group,
4255 West Touhy Avenue,
Lincolnwood (Chicago), Illinois 60646-1975.

Library of Congress Catalog Card Number: 85-63834
International Standard Book Number: 0-8442-3133-9
(Paperbound)
0-8442-3134-7
(Hardbound)
Manufactured in the United States of America.

9 0 WK 9 8 7 6 5 4 3 2

Contents

Foreword

Have you ever hated your phone?

Think back. You're sitting cozily, digesting your pasta, sipping your Sanka®—half-mindedly turning through *Time* or *People* or *War and Peace*, when the phone jars you out of your reverie.

You struggle into the kitchen, or the nook or the bedroom, grab it after the seventh ring and hear a scripted voice recite, "Mr. Knoll, Mr. Alexander Knoll?"

Kroll, I correct the automaton.

"Yes, Mr. Knoll, I represent the Land of Plenty American National Insurance Guild, and I'm pleased to tell you that you have been selected to purchase up to $25,000 of whole life insurance without a physical...."

Or— "Mr. Krell, I represent the Great Sam Houston Sinking Well Shelter...."

Or—"Alex, old buddy, haven't seen you since Morey's Bar when we used to slug boilermakers, listen ol' pal, how are you? You may have heard a couple of us are pledging $10,000 each to the class of '59 building fund...."

Of course, you and I have both been harangued and harassed like this. So is it any surprise that even though I spent twenty years making a living by selling in media—television, print, radio—the phrase "telephone marketing" is a non sequitur?

Telephone annoyances, I know about, but "marketing?" I never equated those jangling nuisances with marketing, until, until....Well, that's an interesting story.

In 1978, Young & Rubicam acquired a first-class Direct Marketing agency in Chicago, Stone & Adler. Shortly thereafter, Stone & Adler began working for AT&T Long Lines in Bedminster, New Jersey. Doing what, I frankly did not know.

As part of my "godfathership" of the agency, I followed Bob Stone, the chairman, over to Bedminster one day to meet his clients. His key client turned out to be John Wyman, vice-president of AT&T Long Lines. I will cut the filler and get to the punch line.

Messrs. Wyman and Stone soon tutored me in the burgeoning but woefully "untapped" (excuse me, I had to try that) potential of "Telemarketing." A new weapon in the nearly stagnant arsenal of marketing.

Soon thereafter, flush with the zeal of a late convert, I took to the stump for Wyman, preaching the gospel of integrated Telemarketing. This was not quite equivalent to Saul's experience on the road to Damascus, but for one who plied the so-called glamour end of the marketing trade for two decades, his was meaningful.

This book grew out of conversations John Wyman and I had in various coffee shops from Carmel to Philadelphia. Let me just quote a bit from that first lecture:

There is a vacuum in selling today—an absence of something—something missing that we used to know and count on. What's missing is the old "neighborhood corner store."

Years ago, in New York, the communications capital of the world, the only phone in many neighborhoods was the "candy store," where people left messages for you with the proprietor.

The "mom and pop" store of yore exists no more.

Over the ghosts of these ghetto gathering places have risen the big, depersonalized, efficient branches of national retailers like Caldor, K-Mart, Zayre, Penney, etc. Gaudy with variety, glutted with goods, at reasonably good prices, they have shucked the "studied carelessness" of the old neighborhood store in favor of end-aisle dumpers, shelf-talkers, over-wire-banners, electronic price scanners and harried gum-chomping checkout clerks.

These automatons have replaced the comfort and intimacy of dealing with an upright tradesman or a storekeeper whose ethics were better than his acumen, whose merchandise and friendship endured, and whose bookkeeping permitted a family to go "on tick" till payday.

That kind of marketing, "one on one," generated a kind of trust that doesn't exist today—but which could exist, could be regenerated. Telemarketing can fill the void of "personal selling" exemplified by the extinction of the corner store.

Electronic contact can become more personal than body contact. How do I know that electronics can be more personal than body contact? A few years ago, we wanted to find out more about this whole nebulous area of "credibility in advertising." Young & Rubicam sponsored some research fielded through the Roper organization, and found this: *Credibility* varies in direct proportion to accessibility of the seller. The closer to home, the nearer the advertiser to the neighborhood, the more likely this message is to be believed.

The reasons for this discrepancy between the believability of a national advertiser and that of a local merchant has nothing to do with the integrity of either.

It's just that the national advertiser is worlds away.

An abstraction.

Unreachable.

The local advertiser is close by.

Reachable.

Touchable.

Punchable.

You get redress.

Roper proved conclusively.

GM exalting its "X" car, or Exxon extolling its Exxonism; in print, TV, whatever—are not as believable as their local dealers, or a local grocer or a local druggist.

If ever a medium demanded *credibility* it is Telemarketing.

If ever one had the potential for more, it's Telemarketing.

That speech was written in 1981.

I now believe Telemarketing will become more and more integrated within the totality of marketing strategy, and that telephone strategies will be built with an eye toward enhancing the overall "personality" or "character" of the brand.

A brand's "personality"—the sum and substance of prospects' feelings about the brand—is a compelling selling tool, if it is consistently managed. Part of managing it is coordinating every nuance of communication—be it in print ads, TV commercials, or telephone conversation—to give the prospect a consistent and positive and personal feeling about the brand, service, or company.

We are on the verge of something Lester Wunderman, chairman of Wunderman, Ricotta & Kline, calls "relationship" marketing or "curriculum" marketing. Where the direct and indirect media will all work together to "teach" a prospect to want and buy a product or service. Telemarketing is an integral part of building the relationship.

What Stone and Wyman delineate in this unique book is the very antithesis of harangue and harassment. The authors have accorded status to the telephone as a *medium* alongside print, radio, TV, direct mail and catalogs. And they should. They show concrete examples of how the phone can increase the efficiency level of all the other media.

With documented case histories you will learn how even a faraway and "faceless" corporation can be given a friendly face. A heart. A soul. A voice.

You will learn how to make Telemarketing the powerful ally of the company sales force, distributor sales force, and multiply that force without adding people.

In their exuberance the authors have not overlooked the reason why you are about to read this book.

PROFIT.

Telemarketing, like all direct response media, is measurable. Measurable down to the last phone call. You are given the guidelines for conducting tests, worksheets for capturing real costs and income. And all the forms you may ever need.

In the end, this book tells you how to increase your company's market value with your customers. Your ongoing customer. Your could-be customer. Your dealers and distributors.

At the end of 1984, Young & Rubicam was entrusted by its clients to place over $3 billion in media around the world.

One of the lessons you learn, in executing that trust most effectively, is that there is a common craving among consumers today from the United States to Europe to Asia. Each one of them wants to be treated like a person. A one and only. Not a number or part of a mass. To the degree that commercial communication can do that—it can enhance their self-esteem and it succeeds.

Clearly, this book demonstrates a clear route—or an architectural plan—for building the personal and friendly atmosphere of the old "neighborhood corner store" into your marketing program.

When Stone and Wyman set out to write this book they had a strenuous mission: To produce the one essential book that can help anyone succeed with Telemarketing.

Having reviewed this manuscript as it developed, I believe they have accomplished their mission.

Alex Kroll, President
Young & Rubicam, Inc.

Successful Telemarketing

Opportunities and Techniques for Increasing Sales and Profits

CHAPTER I

The Scope
of Telemarketing

Two-five-one. Three-nine-two-seven. She knew the phone number as well as her own. Yet—till now—she never had the courage to punch the magic numbers.

"Hello, Tim. This is Karen." *A slight tremor in her young voice.* "Karen Gillick. How are you?—You've been made captain of the varsity. Wow!" *I've got to learn more about football quick.*

"Tell you what I called about, Tim. Our spring prom is coming up. And I thought, Tim … well, I thought maybe you'd like to be my date."

Before Tim could answer, Karen fired three quick salvos. "It's going to be held at the country club. The girls buy the bids. I'd be so proud to escort the captain of the football team.

"Yes, Tim … it will be formal. You'll look great in a tux—you'll go? Super!" As Karen returned her pink Princess phone to its cradle, her joyous squeal reverberated throughout the house. A sale had been made. Euphoria reigned supreme.

Was Karen practicing Telemarketing in its totality? Of course not. Her approach was intuitive. She was driven by massive doses of adrenalin. But she was engaged in *consultative selling*, even though she didn't know it.

And she was using the right words and phrases, even though she didn't know that either; "I thought maybe you'd like to be my date" (a proposition); "It's going to be held at the country club" (a selling point); "The girls buy the bids" (a benefit); "I'd be so proud to escort the captain of the football team" (sincere flattery). In short, Karen was using the most common instrument in all the world— the telephone—to make a sale.

Moving from this poignant experience, we look in on the Chicago suburban parish house of Father Devitt, a holy man to be sure, but a man with a dearth of knowledge or sense about business matters, a Barry Fitzgerald of *Going My Way* in every way.

It's late fall and the good Father Devitt has called an emergency meeting of his Men's Advisory Council. Clearing his throat, he said, "Men, we've got a problem." (Hardly a new situation.) "The furnace is busted and with winter coming on I don't know what we're going to do." "How much will it cost to fix the furnace, Father?" "The man said $20,000." "Good God!"

Typically, some of the council members suggested a raffle, a fall football dance and bingo (of course!) to solve the problem. The head of the council—Gil Kelly—responded by saying, "We just had a raffle for a car, the spring dance raised only $4,500, and the bishop has nixed bingo. Right, Father?" "Right, Gil."

"You guys are going at it all wrong," Gil told the group. "But first, Father, can you give us a list of what each family contributes each week?" "Well, I can give you a list of what each family who uses envelopes gives each week. Those who don't use envelopes drop in a dollar bill or nickels, dimes, and quarters. Some slugs always show up."

"Forget the nickel and dimers, Father. As long as you've got a list of families that will tell us what they contribute each week, I've got a plan that should raise the $20,000."

Turning to his fellow council members, Gil Kelly said, "Here's my plan, guys. As soon as we get the weekly contributors' list from Father Devitt, we'll break it down into categories: those who give $2 to $5 a week; those who give $5 to $10 a week; those who give $10 to $25 a week, and so on.

"Then we'll form a telephone team, breaking down the parish family contributor list so that each team member is assigned 20 families. Each team member will know how much each family customarily contributes each week before he calls.

"Not everyone can give the same amount. So I'd suggest we ask for another dollar a week from those in the $2 to $5 category; $2 extra from the $5 to $10 category; $3 extra from the $10 to $25 category, and an extra $5 a week from those who normally contribute over $25 a week.

"Then, of course, we've got a few biggies," Gil continued. "Hell, I understand old Jim O'Connor, the contractor with the big house on the lake, gave Mayor Daley five grand when he ran for his fifth term. Let me handle that one personally. I'll hit Jim for an extra hundred bucks a week." "My goodness," said Father Devitt.

Did Gil Kelly's plan raise the $20,000? Of course! The church was warm as toast throughout the winter as a result. But was this a Telemarketing plan? In its simplest form—yes.

Kelly didn't have the slightest idea that he was dealing with a "marketing mix," as the professors at Harvard term it. Actually, he was dealing with the four basic elements or channels of distribution of a marketing mix known widely as the "4-Ps"—Product, Price, Promotion, and Place.

Let's see how the 4-Ps were applied against the venerable Father Devitt's dilemma.

Product: Technically, the product was a furnace that would perform the way a furnace should perform. However, in terms of *selling benefits*, the product was warmth and comfort for the parishioners.

Price: Gil Kelly had an unusual problem: What "price" should one "charge" for warmth and comfort? His answer involved a unique strategy: Ask for an amount consistent with the amount that parishioners contribute each week.

Promotion: Kelly had a number of marketing promotion options: a raffle, a dance, bingo, a telephone program. He chose a telephone program. Indeed, he also had the option of composing a letter to go out over the signature of Father Devitt as a promotion vehicle.

Place: Channels of distribution for selling the "product"—warmth and comfort—were the telephone communicators he assigned to his team.

But dealing with the 4-Ps was not the whole story. Having a data base—a list of contributors with meaningful data about them—is what made the plan work effectively. (See Chapter 8.) Naturally, Gil Kelly never heard of a "database."

Well, we've seen the magic of the telephone for a teenager and the power of a Telemarketing program, albeit small and localized, for a harassed pastor, but isn't Telemarketing practiced most often by business firms? Yes. Yes, indeed.

There's a prestigious men's store in Kansas City, Missouri. Jack Henry is its name. It has been in its Plaza location for about a thousand years. At least, so it seems. It caters to the gentry of Kansas City; sons preceded by fathers, preceded by grandfathers. The very rich—lots of cattle money—the well-to-do, the financially comfortable. The famous: Harry Truman, our thirty-third president, a haberdasher by background, knew the store well. And some infamous: Legend has it that the Mayor of Kansas City—"Boss" Pendergast—bought his French-cuffed white shirts there.

Well, the truth is that Jack Henry doesn't really practice Telemarketing. But one of its long-time salesmen does. That could only be Willie. Willie Potts. Willie is affable, even lovable. He stands about five feet four inches tall.

The income of Willie Potts is a closely guarded secret, but if the clothes he wears—it's true that he gets them at a "store discount"— are any clue, Willie does mighty well. His "system" for success is so simple, one has to wonder why all clothing salesmen don't do what Willie does.

Willie maintains a meticulous database (there's that term again) for all his regular customers on $3'' \times 5''$ cards. Let's listen in on what is the prototype of a typical phone conversation between Willie and one of his customers.

"Hello, Martin. This is Willie. Yeah … Willie Potts. —Feeling great. How does Donna like living in Virginia with her new husband, the lawyer?" (Willie's data flagged the fact that Martin's daughter Donna had married a lawyer six months before and that they had moved to Virginia.)

"Is Dorothy still doing charity work at the hospital? —Great. You must be proud of her." (Willie had previously noted that Martin's wife was doing charity work at the hospital.)

"Tell you what I called you about. Our shipment of winter suits just came in yesterday. I got in early this morning before the store opened and went through the racks. I couldn't believe it, Martin. There was a suit that I swear was made just for you.

"You know how you like extra deep pockets. Well, you could empty out your desk drawers in these. And I know you have to operate with two sets of glasses. Well, I tried my glasses in the handkerchief pocket and they fit just right.

"And I checked the trousers. I know you've got a small watermelon in the front and a little rumble seat in the rear. No problem. There's extra-wide seams. Plenty of room to let out. You know that Phil, the best tailor we've ever had, has all your measurements. Alterations will be no problem.

"Sure there's a vest. Just the style you like. Four pockets and an adjustable strap.

"This suit is lightweight, 100% wool. The thinnest of pin stripes. Very similar to the brown summer suit you bought in June.

"This suit is the exact shade of blue you like—size 42? Right. Martin, when I saw this suit I took it right off the rack and locked it in the back room so no one can see it till you get in here. When can you come?

"Thursday night at 6:00. I'll be here for sure. And Martin—if Dorothy can make it, please bring her along. See you Thursday night at 6:00. Bye."

What a database! Willie knows the name of Martin's daughter, when she got married, what her husband does, where she lives. He knows the name of Martin's wife, and knows her extracurricular activity. He knows the type of coat pockets Martin prefers, the fact that he needs a handkerchief pocket that will accommodate a second set of glasses, that the front and back of trousers have to be let out, that he likes a vest with an adjustable strap, that he likes lightweight wool suits for winter, what he bought last, that he likes thin pin stripes, what shade of blue he likes, and his size. And the *piece de resistance*: Willie knows that if he can get Dorothy to come in with Martin his sale is almost assured because this is exactly the type of suit Dorothy likes on Martin!

The big question is—can Willie Potts' success be multiplied? Absolutely. Not only within one store, but within a chain of stores across a nation. The wonders of telecommunication equipment and systems, the efficiency of computers and computer programs makes Telemarketing feasible for retail chains, wholesalers, manufacturers, distributors, and service organizations. Application possibilities boggle the mind.

TELEMARKETING DEFINED

But before we look at a few thumbnail sketches of true Telemarketing applications, let's first define Telemarketing.

Telemarketing comprises the integrated and systematic application of telecommunications and information processing technologies with management systems to optimize the marketing communications mix used by a company to reach its customers. It retains personalized customer interaction while simultaneously attempting to better meet customer needs and improve cost effectiveness.

The foregoing is the technical definition of Telemarketing, but here's a more succinct definition.

Telemarketing is a new marketing discipline that utilizes telecom-munications technology as part of a well-planned, organized, and managed marketing program that prominently features the use of personal selling, using non-face-to-face contacts.

Telemarketing can substitute for some of the marketing communi-cations mix and supplement others. But to maximize the impact of Telemarketing, the marketer should mix and match Telemarketing with the total advertising and promotion program.

Now let's take a look at a cross-section of firms who are mixing and matching successfully.

TELEMARKETING SUCCESS STORIES

Mention the name White Castle to anyone who grew up in the eight midwestern states and their immediate response is "hamburgers." Two other words follow— "ten cents."

This nostalgic recall quickly reaches the taste buds: a nice, fat, juicy sizzling hamburger coming off the grill, slapped on a warm bun, sprinkled with fresh chopped onions, covered with pickle slices, and topped off with a generous amount of Snyder's catsup. (Those were the "good old days.")

Well, the youth of the 1940s grew up, as all generations must. In a mobile America, thousands migrated outside of the White Castle trading area. They took their hankering for White Castle hamburgers with them. To this day, they continue to satisfy their appetites for the hamburger of their youth—thanks to Telemarketing.

The magazine *Advertising Age* updated this unique marketing story in their May 9, 1983 issue. Picking up on the chain's cult following, a TV campaign is being aired with the theme "White Castle has the taste some people won't live without." Viewers are given an 800 toll-free number—1-800-W CASTLE—to learn how their lingering taste for White Castle hamburgers can be satisfied wherever they reside.

Reflecting upon the Telemarketing program, Gail Turley, White Castle's advertising and PR manager, said, "Right now, just with word-of-mouth advertising, we're shipping 10,000 hamburgers a week. We're converting 17% of inquiries to orders, which is lower than we expected, but there's still a huge curiosity factor involved." Minimum order is fifty hamburgers for $57. (The 10-cent hamburger is dead, but White Castle lives on!) The phone dialogue with prospects and customers, we might add, gives White Castle an opportunity to build a unique database for future action and an opportunity for market research as well.

The mini case histories continue.

American Express Merchandise Services handles approximately 2.5 million orders a year. Fifty percent of those are received by phone and the percentage of phone orders is increasing. The merchandise ranges from plain high ticket items to fancy high tech products. Eight years after the Telemarketing program began, American Express had increased sales from $29 million to more than $200 million.

Budget Rent a Car's Reservations Center handles more than 20,000 calls a day with over 200 agents. Budget is experiencing over 20% increases in reservations worldwide.

Beech-Nut Nutrition Corporation features a hotline with an 800 number that parents can call to get information on child development, nutrition, and prenatal and postnatal care. The Telemarketing Center has many prerecorded tapes on a variety of child health topics one or more of which are played for incoming callers after the nature of their inquiry is determined. They also have a reference library to research other questions. They average about 300 calls a day, with a volume of approximately 80,000 calls a year.

Clairol prints an 800 number on all of its hair-coloring packages and instruction inserts. Customers are invited to call for information about product selection and use. Over 500,000 calls are answered each year.

B. F. Goodrich uses Telemarketing to help establish itself as a leader in the chemical industry because of high-quality service. Its Telemarketing program has helped to reduce its sales/ordering costs by roughly $250,000 in one year.

Kelly-Springfield Tire Company, with its Telemarketing center in place over five years, claims the center has become an important and strategic part of its recent sales surge.

Signature Financial/Marketing, Inc. (The Signature Group), the Telemarketer of consumer clubs and services and a multiline insurer for Montgomery-Ward and Co., Inc., has an outbound telephone program that makes more than four million outbound calls annually for club memberships and other services. In addition, its 800 number is featured in all insurance advertising and policyholder communications. In one year, more than 500,000 calls were received.

Olan Mills, a family-owned chain of photography studios, uses Telemarketing to set up appointments for sittings. Years ago, it replaced its door-to-door sales staff with a phone operation. Prior to the switchover, the company had thirty studios. Today, it has over 900 studios with over $200 million a year in sales.

Quaker Oats, in a creative promotion for one of its cereal brands, utilized a toll-free number in a sweepstakes promotion. More than 24 million calls were received, and market share for the cereal increased 33% during the promotion period. (See Chapter 5.)

Raleigh Bicycles uses Telemarketing to reduce the high cost of face-to-face selling and to improve relations with its dealers. The Telemarketing sales specialists support the outside sales force and provide an instant and constant communication link between Raleigh and its dealers. Sparsely located dealers are handled via Telemarketing, thereby reducing travel costs but maintaining excellent sales and service to accounts.

Scotts Lawn Care uses a hotline to answer customer questions about the proper use of its garden products. In operation since 1972, the Telemarketing Center has already received over one million calls for information.

Valvoline is using Telemarketing to differentiate products, improve customer service, and increase productivity. Ninety percent of the company's orders are received by telephone. The average order runs about $10,000.

Whirlpool puts an 800 number on every appliance, warranty, use and care guide, and in all its sales literature. Customers are encouraged to call with questions or problems. The company estimates that in 1983 it saved its customers about three-quarters of a million dollars on repair and service calls. The company itself saved over $500,000 on unnecessary visits to customers who were still under warranty.

Digital Equipment Corporation uses Telemarketing for order processing. Its catalogs generate about 15,000 calls a month for computer peripherals and supplies. The company has said that its market is expanding so rapidly that without Telemarketing, it would not be able to keep up with the expansion.

Goldbergs' Marine caters to the boating market through catalogs and retail stores. Fifty percent of the business comes in over the phone via a toll-free number: 1-800-BOATING. Telemarketing is an invaluable tool in selling big ticket items because a customer can ask questions about the equipment for which the advertising copy does not provide enough detail.

THE CHANGING BUSINESS ENVIRONMENT

The mini case histories that we have just presented are represent-ative of the multitudenous applications of Telemarketing. Telemarketing is so much more than telephone selling: at its finest, it is customer communication integrated with total marketing programs.

There is a hunger today for recognition and personal attention. The computer age has relegated both the consumer and business people to *impersonal contact.* How often have you, the reader, in a state of complete frustration, exploded with— "I'm damn sick and tired of trying to talk to a stupid computer."

Yet business executives find themselves in a catch-22 situation: In most cases, they can no longer afford field sales calls to resolve problems and retain customer goodwill. The telephone—Telemarket-ing—fulfills the thirst for personal attention and solves the cost problem as well. Indeed, Telemarketing is an integral part of a dramatic change in the business environment.

Let us zero in on the changing business environment. From the smallest to the largest, we find that virtually every business is affected by today's changing life styles, shortages of capital, and high interest rates. These factors have all changed the way we do business.

Some of the changes confronting business are external. The challenge for business executives is to find ways to adapt to and to accommodate these changes—and to capitalize on them.

Prominent among the external forces is the change in the makeup of the American workforce. The number of working women is increasing and rapidly exceeding 50% of the total labor force. In addition, there has been a steady rise in the number of both men and women living alone— single person households.

Yet, household responsibilities remain. Homes are to be managed, children are to be raised. The roles of income producer and home-maker are now often shared by husband and wife or performed by a single person. This leaves little time to pursue such mundane neces-sities as shopping.

This trend has encouraged more companies to market directly to the consumer. Thus, direct marketing programs have grown—from catalog selling to direct mail and TV offerings to media advertising and bill-enclosure merchandise sales. The growth of credit card availability has encouraged this direct response selling.

The availability of toll-free 800 service also has stimulated direct response selling. Periodical publishers, mail-order houses, department stores, book and record publishers, stationery retailers, home furnishing stores, and credit card companies are some of the industries that sell direct to the consumer. Companies such as Better Homes & Gardens; Book of the Month Club, Inc.; Fortune; Forbes; Fingerhut Corp.; RCA Records; Omaha Steaks International; VISA; and many more market directly to the consumer.

Cost of Sales Calls

The changing consumer environment has been matched by a changing business-to-business environment.

The spiraling cost of sales calls has made Telemarketing an imperative for industrial firms with field sales forces. The following graph, better than words can convey, illustrates the need for Telemarketing as an adjunct to personal selling.

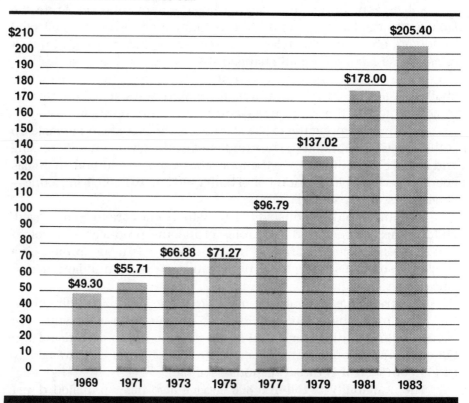

Cost of an Industrial Sales Call

Year	Cost
1969	$49.30
1971	$55.71
1973	$66.88
1975	$71.27
1977	$96.79
1979	$137.02
1981	$178.00
1983	$205.40

It is startling to note that it cost $205.40 for the average industrial sales call in 1983, according to a continuing study by McGraw-Hill. Ten years earlier, the cost of that sales call was $66.88. That's an increase of almost 3½ times!

The high cost of field sales calls is particularly devastating when servicing marginal accounts. A case in point is A. B. Dick, a leading manufacturer of duplicating and copying machines as well as supplies.

In 1973, the cost of a call by an industry salesperson was $66.88. Research disclosed that the average order for supplies was only $50. And there were over 100,000 customers in this category. A. B. Dick faced a dilemma. Either they would have to abort supply sales to this large segment of their customer base, thus giving the business by default to local supply dealers offering competitive brands, or they would have to find a way to sell this customer category in a more cost-efficient way. A. B. Dick, smart marketers that they are, sought a more cost-efficient way.

A direct-marketing test program incorporating Telemarketing was devised by their advertising agency, Stone & Adler. It was a three-prong program:

1. Integral to the program was a telephone sales service. Branch offices would phone supplies customers on a regularly scheduled basis to solicit supply orders and answer any questions about supplies and equipment.

2. Periodic mailings would be made to the list of marginal customers, making special time-limited offers.

3. A new all-inclusive supplies and equipment catalog would be prepared, making it easy for the marginal customer to order by phone or by mail.

Several test markets were selected for the program. Results from the Boston test market will suffice to illustrate the success of the Telemarketing aspect of the program.

Result	Percentage of Total
Immediate orders	10.1
Future calls requested	46.2
Asked for salesperson's visit	8.8
Required special handling	6.6
Not interested	28.3

An unexpected bonus was new equipment sales. Those who requested a sales visit purchased some $10,000 in new equipment within three weeks of the completion of the Boston calling program. The changing business environment has dictated that scores of original equipment manufacturers investigate Telemarketing as a cost-efficient way to service their aftermarkets.

THE CUSTOMER'S SALES CYCLE

The scope of Telemarketing applications varies by types of companies, of course. But in exploring the extent of scope it's a good idea to review the eight selling stages followed by most marketing organizations.

We generally think of the eight stages as hierarchical and that each stage is a prerequisite for the next. They can be shown as a hierarchy of effects model*.

*Patterned after Lavidge & Steiner's "Hiearchy of Effects" Model

Not all companies' sales cycles include each individual step. In some cases, a few may be combined into a single step. But, whether the organization is engaged in selling to business or in selling to consumers, most if not all of these steps in the sales cycle are involved—individually or in combination—and are incorporated into the act of selling.

Different industries fulfill each of the steps in the sales cycle with different communication vehicles (e.g., print and TV advertising, direct mail, field sales).

There are many ways that Telemarketing can be used to support and/or replace field selling. To learn where, let us take the eight steps in the sales cycle and identify each in terms of five levels of interest—account calls that are nonrevenue producers (service calls), calls made with accounts that are only marginally profitable (revenue in relation to the cost of the sales call), and primary accounts that demand and deserve attention from field salespeople plus the levels of high-cost and low-cost products. The following matrix illustrates this identification process.

Integrating Telemarketing into the Sales Cycle*

	Educate-Awareness	Inquiry	Infor-mation	Sales Desire Response	Proposal	Close Sale	Follow-Up	Service
Service Calls	T	T	T	T	T	T	T	T
Marginal Accounts	T	T	T	T	T	T	T	T
Primary Accounts	S	T S	T S	S	S	S	T S	T S
High Ticket Items	T S	T S	T S	T S	S	S	T S	T S
Low Ticket Items	T	T	T	T	T	T	T	T

T = Telemarketing   S = Salesperson

*Reprinted with permission of American Telephone and Telegraph—Copyright 1983 AT&T.

Note how Telemarketing can be an ideal communications vehicle for moving prospects through many of the steps in the sales cycle. In exploring the opportunities, consider where Telemarketing might be used to support or substitute for other vehicles, particularly the field salesperson.

As you can see in the matrix, the face-to-face visit can be targeted for priority assignments. On the other hand, a Telemarketing Center can be assigned all service calls and can be called upon to displace the field salesperson in handling marginal accounts. In addition, Telemarketing Centers can supplement field salespeople in serving primary accounts.

Although handling nonrevenue calls becomes an expense that the account may not have borne before, it is low in relation to the cost of in-person visits. It becomes profitable as it uncovers qualified leads, assists in supplementing the salesperson's visits, and opens an opportunity to sell once the customer's problem is resolved.

In the case of marginal accounts and low ticket items, a Telemarketing Center can receive inquiries, provide information, receive customer response, offer a proposal, close the sale, follow up, and provide answers to product problems.

With primary and high ticket items, Telemarketing specialists can supplement salespeople at many steps in the sales cycle. For example, customer inquiries often can be satisfied over the telephone, and information can be provided orally if that suits the customer's need. And for a follow-up after the sale, the telephone is a natural.

By viewing the sales cycle as a series of linked steps, you can pinpoint where Telemarketing can fit and how it can work alone or in concert with a face-to-face sales force.

THE SPECTRUM OF TELEMARKETING APPLICATIONS

Another way to explore Telemarketing opportunities is to look at a Telemarketing sales continuum as a means to identifying applications.

Order taking usually begins with a catalog or other promotion mailed to potential customers. The prospect is encouraged to use the convenience of calling an 800 number to place an order.

Telemarketing Sales Continuum

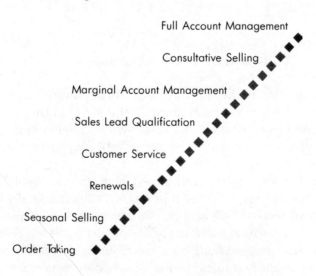

For example, when Fotomat introduced a new product—videotape sales and rentals—it publicized an 800 number for customers to place orders and to get directions to the nearest local Fotomat Hut.

Additionally, an order-taking operation offers the possibility of upgrading by including limited cross-selling, new product couponing, and even simple marketing research.

Seasonal selling is another Telemarketing application. The Swim Shop—a company in Nashville, Tennessee, that supplies gear to summer swim teams—offers an example of how to extend a limited sales season. Since the peak swimming season lasts about twelve weeks—too short a period for the shop to rely on traditional methods to fill orders—it made available an 800 number so orders could be received and filled promptly late in the season. Avoiding the mail stretched out the firm's sales season.

Renewals are another widely used aspect of Telemarketing. These applications are now an integral part of a magazine's circulation subscription program. One phone call can produce what it might take several subscription renewal letters to accomplish. The technique has been used successfully also for selling other products—fruit, cheese, even plants.

As a major user of Telemarketing for policy renewals, one insurance company's "conservation program" saves about $20,000 per month by using Telemarketing to conserve policies about to lapse.

Customer service, another area for improved effectiveness and cost control, is the next step up the Telemarketing continuum. Using a unique system, the 3M Company offers an 800 number to assist their telecommunication equipment customers. The 3M National Service Center, located in St. Paul, Minnesota, is manned 365 days a year, 24 hours a day, with skilled technicians and coordinators. Through systematic questioning and a variety of facsimile, ASCII communication terminals, store and forward electronic message distribution terminals, the latest electronic monitoring and testing equipment, and a sophisticated on-line computer system, the staff can isolate the failure to an equipment problem or operator error. The 3M center has found that on more than 30% of the calls, the equipment failure can be solved in minutes, without dispatching a service technician.

Sales lead qualification is designed to reduce the number of wasted in-person sales visits. With an estimated $205 average for each industrial sales call, companies cannot afford to send salespeople to unqualified prospects. The better qualified a prospect is, the greater the sales call's potential for success. When a prospect is prequalified by telephone, Telemarketing helps to direct outside salespeople to where the highest sales potential exists.

Reliance Electric, a Cleveland-based manufacturer of electric and mechanical power distribution equipment and weighing scales and systems, uses Telemarketing to qualify half of the 125,000 sales leads received annually. Because almost all sales require customized products, Reliance's field sales force of 700, are all highly trained engineers; Reliance utilizes Telemarketing to focus their sales team on new business potential.

By incorporating an 800 number into all of its advertising, Reliance generates lead responses into its Telemarketing center—called the Marketing Information Center. Telemarketing specialists qualify these prospects—notifying field sales of the "hot" prospects for follow-up within twenty-four hours. Reliance also utilizes outbound WATS follow-up to qualify nontelephone generated leads (i.e., letters, reply cards, trade show contacts, and so on). The M.I.C. system, in its first year of operation, increased quotation activity of field sales by one million dollars. In its second year, Reliance is expecting that figure to further increase by 50%.

Marginal account management allows a marketer to capitalize on the revenue potential of smaller accounts without the high cost burden of face-to-face sales visits. Banding together marginal accounts spread over a wide geographic area permits profitable coverage at low cost.

To handle such targeted accounts profitably, Hallmark Cards, Inc., the social expression company, uses Telemarketing. Hallmark uses a combination of direct mail and Telemarketing to give its remote outlets the same highly personal, current card selection as any urban, large card shop or department store.

Consultative selling is a highly personal involved sales technique. With Telemarketing, a customer's needs are probed by a specially trained sales representative. Personalized solutions are designed during the phone contact, when possible. An ideal example is the AT&T National Sales Center (described in Chapter 3).

Full account management is at the very zenith of the marketing spectrum. It involves order taking, answering questions about order status, inventory availability, shipment scheduling and billing, credit checking and product consultation. This full-service operation includes both selling and customer service.

The full scope of Telemarketing is a far cry from the instinctive application of our exuberant teenager, or the impromptu plan of the advisers to the venerable Father Devitt, or even the structured plan of the lovable Willie Potts. Yet, using the telephone as a part of the marketing mix is as natural as Karen Gillick phoning her football hero, Gil Kelly and his council members phoning Father Devitt's parishioners, or Willie Potts phoning his customers with database information in hand.

Putting it all together, making the most of the opportunities is what all the chapters that follow are about.

CHAPTER 2

The GE
Answer Center™

"We've paid for 160,000 phone calls last month. Within three months, we hope to be paying for 180,000 calls a month!"

With this improbable statement—every word is true—we introduce one of the most spectacular communication and customer service stories in American business—The GE Answer Center™.

A short distance from the Louisville, Kentucky, airport we come upon two Georgian-style buildings, buildings that take us back in history to Williamsburg, Virginia, where George Washington, Patrick Henry, and other founding fathers led genteel lives, communicating in an unhurried and caring way. It is significant that the home address of the GE Answer Center™ is 9500 Williamsburg Plaza, the Patrick Henry Building.

Home of The GE Answer Center.™

As we enter the "home" and proceed through the foyer, we enter the reception area with its soft carpeting and richly paneled walls. We are greeted by a pleasant receptionist with the warm smile of Mrs. Ulmer. Mrs. Ulmer is sewing a button on a jacket. "We have a visitor who has a loose button and we aim to please," she explains with a smile. "What can we do for you?" she asks. "Mr. Powell Taylor, please."

However, before we meet Powell Taylor, let's listen to Dick Van Patten, spokesperson for GE, giving a capsulized explanation of The GE Answer Center™ in a movie GE has prepared for their employees and dealers as well as for teachers and consumer groups.

Hello, everybody, I'm Dick Van Patten and I've got good news for you. The folks at GE realize that things are tough these days and the buyer has to be more discriminating than ever. So they came up with the idea of The GE Answer Center, which is really a friendly way of doing business. There's nothing to buy. No sales pitch. Just a place consumers can call toll-free 24 hours a day, 7 days a week and ask questions about products before or after they buy them.

As Powell Taylor, manager of The Answer Center, pointed out to me, before a person buys a product they want to know what's available, what model and feature choices there are, and where they can actually buy the product. The Answer Center answers all these questions on any GE consumer product.

On the other hand, after the person has bought and owns a GE product they may need to get information on how to use it, maintain it properly, or fix it if it breaks down. The Answer Center can give the consumer the answers to all these questions too.

GE wants consumers to feel that the company stands behind its products. They're not going to leave the consumer as soon as the product is purchased. Instead, GE is just a phone call away with any help that may be needed. It's a new concept and, when you think about it, it's really nice to see GE giving the consumer something they can really use.

Now let's take a tour of The Answer Center and answer a few questions of our own, like how it works. First, when a call comes into The Answer Center it is directed by a computer to a consumer specialist who will answer such questions as what to buy, where to buy it, how to use the product or how to get service or repair it yourself.

These highly trained representatives complete a 160-hour training session before they're ready to help you. And they are trained on a recurring basis to keep up on the latest product features. They have instant access to the largest centralized consumer product database of its kind in the world. So in seconds she can recall a great deal of information on just about anything that has to do with GE products.

When The Answer Center was tested in certain markets, it handled about 2,000 calls a week. Now with The Answer Center in full operation, they expect to handle more than 40,000 a week or more than two million calls annually.

Now if the questions are more complex such as how to remove and replace a heating unit of the oven, well then the call is referred to technical specialists in another section of The Answer Center. These people are well trained in performing actual maintenance. Like the consumer specialist, they have a great deal of data that they can recall on the screen such as parts listings, diagrams of circuits, even information on older models of GE appliances. It's all here in The Answer Center.

And there is even a third area for anybody who has very technical questions on things such as GE made jet engines or other highly technical questions. In that case, the questions are referred to a special research section and they generally have an answer back within 24 hours.

As you can see, The Answer Center has all bases covered when it comes to answering questions about GE products. No question is too small or too complex for The Answer Center. Someone even called to find out the name and composer of the music for the GE lightbulb commercial. So the consumer specialists take care of questions about GE products and services. The technical specialists are always ready to help answer more complex questions about the operational features of the products. And the research section of The Answer Center is prepared to research even the most specific questions and return an answer within 24 hours.

The Answer Center has been four years in planning and is already meeting the goals it set out to accomplish. One—to open a personal dialogue between the consumer and GE. Two—to provide the consumer with helpful information and expertise. And three—to build consumer confidence in GE. And that's just what The Answer Center is doing.

From surveys on The Answer Center GE found a 95% rate of satisfaction with consumers who had used The Answer Center. Oh, just take a look at some of the responses from consumers across the country.

"Dear Sir, this is a fan letter. I wanted you to know that I have used your GE Answer Center with great results. I've told friends about it and suggested that they use it to help make purchasing decisions as

I did. P.S. May I add that every person I've talked to at the Center acts like a friend."

"Dear Sir, I would like to thank General Electric and Jane Simpson in particular for your courteous and extremely helpful service. In an age where a customer is often made to feel like an annoying intruder, it was a pleasure to come in contact with a charming, courteous person like Jane Simpson."

"To the Management. Our refrigerator, now 13 years old, gave out after a Saturday night party. I wanted to thank your company for having help available, especially on Sunday."

Well, as you can see everybody is very excited about The Answer Center. It's a new concept, a new idea, and it's built totally on the premise of helping people. No matter who you are, if you're involved with GE or their products in any way you profit from The Answer Center.

THE "FATHER" AND THE "FAMILY"

"Mr. Taylor is ready for you." With this, the manager of the Center extended his welcome with a warm smile and firm handshake. If The GE Answer Center™ story were cast in Hollywood, the casting director would surely seek out a Lorne Greene (Ben Cartwright) to play the role of Powell Taylor.

Handsome in a masculine way. Immaculately groomed, an authority figure. Steeped in wisdom and GE experience. Respected, but not feared—Powell Taylor leads not with an iron fist, but with gentle reins. He gives authority to each consumer consultant; he counsels them as necessary. Powell Taylor is the head of a mature family in every way.

Putting us at ease in his warm and comfortably appointed office, Powell Taylor proceeded to spin the yarn of the GE saga in a fascinating and unhurried manner.

THE GENESIS OF THE CONCEPT

The whole notion of a free telephone service was the result of studies conducted several years ago when GE set up task forces to look into consumer needs and interests. (Mr. Taylor was a member of one of the task forces.)

Findings revealed that while consumers were happy that major corporations in all industries were providing them with product

Powell Taylor and receptionist welcoming visitors.

information, the increased sophistication and added features in many products meant longer and more complicated use and care instructions.

Commenting on their findings, Taylor explained, "Our research showed that people want to cut through all that information, that they want to find out what they need to know without having to read through thirty pages.

"Today's consumer is not like the old consumer. There are more working wives. And people today are interested in getting more value for their money—in getting quality products. The GE Answer Center™ was created in direct response to these findings. Our program is in tune with the whole new consumer expectation of getting quality products, of being able to gain access to a company, of being able to 'talk' to a company.

"GE is a big corporation," Taylor continued, "and in the past it may have seemed faceless to its customers. This program gives GE a personality—people can call up and talk to someone. It actually takes this large company and makes it a small one in dealing with the consumer. It brings GE into a personal relationship with its customers.

"GE now has the advantages of what it can offer the consumer through being a large company as well as the advantages of a small company because the customer has access to GE just as he would to a small neighborhood store. What we now have is a high tech company with *high touch*," Taylor continued.

"The goals the company set out to achieve, based upon our research, were three: (1) to build a personal dialogue between the consumer and GE, (2) to provide the consumer with helpful information and expertise, and (3) to build consumer confidence in GE."

"A few questions, Powell. When did you start to test The Answer Center concept?" "We started in June 1981 in four test cities—Baltimore, Denver, New Orleans, and Portland." "When did you go national?" "In June of 1982." "How many consumer calls did your Center handle in 1983?" "About 1.4 million." "Wow!"

"The scope of the Center is slightly incredible, but what were the major things you had to do to make it work?" "We had two major objectives: (1) to develop a database of information that would make it possible for consumer service people to answer any question asked about our 120 product lines with 8,500 models, and (2) to develop a staff with good interpersonal skills to deal with the consumer."

DEVELOPING THE DATABASE

Eleven thousand manhours went into the development of the database. In order to be able to answer every conceivable question relating to the 120 product lines, 500,000 pieces of data were put into the computer. And the data is updated constantly.

The questions pour in twenty-four hours a day, seven days a week, at the rate of over forty thousand a week. "I want to buy a new refrigerator. But there are so many available. What would be best for my family?" With the touch of a keyboard, the consumer representative ties into the computer and calls up the needed information on his/her terminal video screen. (See Exhibit 2.1.)

"How do I clean an electric drip coffee maker?"

"Where can I get GE Factory Service?"

"I want to install central air conditioning. What size unit will I need for a 2,500 square foot, five-room house?"

"We're renovating our kitchen. What kind of financing is available from General Electric?"

```
PKK
CIO1I M TFF24RC
             NUM OF SOLUTIONS    12
CIO2I MABG/REFRIGERATOR/SIDE-BY-SIDE/MOD-TFF24RC                    NOS ***MORE***

FEATURES:

* FRESH FOOD CAPACITY (CU. FT.)          - 14.93 CU. FT.
* FREEZER CAPACITY (CU. FT.)             - 8.57 CU. FT.
* SHELF AREA (SQ. FT.)                   - 30.7 SQ. FT.
* REFRIGERATOR CABINET SHELVES           - 5 TOTAL
* ADJUSTABLE SHELVES                     - 4 GLASS
* MEAT OR SEALED SNACK PACK              - SEALED SNACK PACK PLUS
                                           ADJUSTA-TEMP PAN
* VEGETABLE / FRUIT BIN(S)               - 3 (2 SEALED)
* DOOR SHELVES                           - 2 FIXED & 3 ADJUSTABLE BINS
                                           PLUS DAIRY COMPARTMENT
* REMOVEABLE WINE / FRUIT RACK           - YES
* FREEZER COMPARTMENT SHELVES            - 4 ADJUSTABLE EPOXY-COATED
                                           WIRE PLUS SLIDE-OUT BIN
* EXTERIOR WATER / ICE SERVICE           - WATER, ICE, CRUSHED ICE &
                                           NIGHT LIGHT
* AUTOMATIC ICEMAKER                     - YES
* ICE TRAYS                              - NO

CIO1I M TFF24RC
             NUM OF SOLUTIONS    12
CIO2I MABG/REFRIGERATOR/SIDE-BY-SIDE/MOD-TFF24RC                    NOS

* CABINET LINER MATERIAL                 - ENAMEL ON STEEL
* CABINET INSULATION - POURED POLY FOAM  - YES
* ENERGY SAVER SWITCH                    - AUTOMATIC (CONDENSOR LOOP)
* ADJUSTABLE ROLLERS                     - YES
* REVERSIBLE DOOR SWING                  - NO
* ONYX (BLACK) PANEL KIT AVAILABLE       - YES KIT NO. TFP24R
* COLOR SELECTIONS                       - WHITE, ALMOND, HARVEST,
                                           AVOCADO, & COFFEE
* APPROX. SHIPPING WEIGHT (LBS.)         - 376 LBS.
* ESTIMATED POWER CONSUMPTION (KWH/MO.)  - 147


DIMENSIONS:  HEIGHT - 66 5/8" WIDTH - 35 3/4" DEPTH - 30 1/2"



END OF FILE
```

Exhibit 2.1. Features of a GE refrigerator reprinted from a computer printout.

"I don't understand how to hook up my video cassette recorder. What is the procedure?"

"This has really bugged me. The knob from my radio has disappeared. Where can I get a new one?"

"Our GE range needs a new heating element. I want to repair it myself to save money. Can you assist me?"

"The music for your recent GE lighting commercial was beautiful. What's the name of the melody and who composed it?"

"A friend told me that I could use something called 'Quick Fix' to repair my washer. Can you help me?"

"What's the difference in energy efficiency between a 50-watt and a 100-watt bulb?"

Questions. Questions by the thousands. And the answers are in the computer. In the few cases where the computer is stumped, a GE technical specialist comes to the rescue.

Statistics indicate that calls, on the average, break down into three categories, as follows:

1. Prepurchase calls   25%
2. Use and care of GE equipment   35%
3. Service of GE equipment   40%

The computer contains no information about competitive products...on purpose. Customer service personnel are instructed to suggest courteously that the caller comparison shop when they are asked questions such as, "What's the basic difference between a 17-cubic-foot GE refrigerator and a Frigidaire of the same capacity?"

Thousands of callers inquire about the location of the closest GE dealer for specific product lines. And the computer answers these questions, too—instantly. (See Exhibit 2.2.) As a matter of fact, the CRT displays all of the dealers in the specified area, giving each dealer "a fair shake."

DEVELOPING THE PEOPLE

At the GE Answer Center™, the database is high tech, but the people are high touch. Mention the people—his "family"—and the eyes of Powell Taylor light up like a string of GE Christmas lights. For his people—over 150 strong—are the voice of GE, the human contact between the manufacturer and the consumer.

The criteria for selection, the training program, the atmosphere, the facilities, the motivation, the caring explain more than any one factor why the Center is a world-class model.

Powell Taylor pointed to the people of Disney World—young, clean-cut, squeaky clean, outgoing—as the model the company decided to follow in building the GE Center staff.

"We look for people who are outgoing, bright, poised, and naturally curious. They must be good listeners and be able to think on their feet," Powell said. "We don't want robots," he added. "The consumer representatives are GE's front-line contact with the consumer public. They

```
RECD:U  2959  NORA J HAMILTON     1/12 11:01 R 1/12 11:03
PLEASE PRINT.

60076        STATUS: S/D  REG:  26  ZONE: 09   CODE:  55168   CUSTID:  00088367
SKOKIE                    NORTH SHORE
ILLINOIS                  REFRIGERATION                4001 GOLF ROAD
BR:GE           FRAN:WARR TYP: CC PHONE: 312-583-4100    CATEG: PARTS
PROD LN:REFRG RANGE H.L.   D&D    RAC    T.V.   MISC.
HOURS:MON  9:00 - 21:00  TUE  9:00 - 21:00  WED  9:00 - 21:00
       THU  9:00 - 21:00  FRI  9:00 - 21:00  SAT  9:00 - 21:00 SUN  0:00 -  0:00
TRAVL


60076                      REG:  26  ZONE: 00   CODE:  42009   CUSTID:  00325210
SKOKIE                     POLK BROTHERS               9300 N. SKOKIE BLVD.
ILLINOIS
BR:HP                      PHONE:312 -677-0500    CATEG: RET-MULT
PROD LN:REFRG RANGE H.L.   D&D    RAC    MISC.
HOURS:MON  9:00 - 21:00  TUE  9:00 - 21:00  WED  9:00 - 21:00
       THU  9:00 - 21:00  FRI  9:00 - 21:00  SAT  9:00 - 21:00 SUN  0:00 -  0:00
TRAVL
```

Exhibit 2.2. List of GE dealers in a given ZIP code, reproduced from a computer printout.

must be able to communicate the company's desire to provide service and show interest in the owner or would-be owner of GE products."

The dress code Taylor insists upon for his telephone represent-atives is unique in telephone communications. He tells his staff "Dress exactly as you would if you were visiting a GE customer. The way you feel about your own grooming projects over the phone." And it does. We saw men wearing shirts, ties, and jackets; women wore dresses, skirts and blouses, and tailored slacks.

HIRING CRITERIA

The model staff didn't come about by accident. GE set up specific criteria as follows:

Interpersonal skills

Good speech and grammar

Neutral accent

Typing skills

CRT ability

Interest

Permanency

Flexibility

Neatness

Reviewing the specific criteria, Taylor put particular emphasis upon speech and grammar, accent, permanency, and flexibility, although all criteria must be met to be considered. If a prescreen phone interview indicates phone manner flaws, the interview ends there.

Permanency is a key issue. No part-time workers are accepted. The Center offers full-time employment and will not hire applicants who view employment as less than a career with permanency. Flexibility is key because of the 24-hour-a-day, 7-day-a-week operation. Each applicant is asked frankly, "Is your family situation such that you would feel comfortable working odd hours such as a night shift, Saturdays and Sundays?"

Meeting specific criteria alone is not sufficient to gain employment. Applicants also must rate high against the following strengths:

- Even-tempered
- Intelligent
- Enthusiastic
- Personable
- Problem solver
- Empathetic
- Self-motivated
- Effective listener
- Outgoing
- Poise
- Compassionate
- Sympathetic
- Knowledgeable
- Professional
- "Disney World" type
- Work Experience

In reviewing the specific criteria and strengths required, it's no surprise that out of every 500 applicants only 15 are hired.

Many of the new hires come from recommendations of the staff. And they are very picky about whom they recommend because they are jealous of the quality of their family. About 20% of the new hires come from other GE departments, leaving 80% who are hired from outside the company.

Do their stringent hiring requirements pay off? Certainly they do. Not counting moves to other cities due to a spouse being moved and/or childbearing, turnover is only between one and two percent. An extremely low figure for any industry, but incredible for telephone communications.

THE ANSWER CENTER TRAINING PROGRAM

Once hired, a consumer service person enters an intensive four-week training program. The training program includes sixteen hours of interpersonal communications skills, sixteen hours of familiarization with sophisticated telephone equipment, forty hours on the use of CRTs, learning how to access the GE computer's large database. Another forty-eight hours are spent in structured role-playing sessions with the trainers and in day-long dress rehearsals during which outside GE employees call in and pretend to be customers.

The program would not be complete without learning something about the GE consumer products and services and what makes them tick. That something begins with a twenty-eight-hour basic familiarization course on the inner workings and features of all GE products—from hair dryers and microwave ovens to video equipment and air conditioners. And it goes on and on and on. "Training never stops," Powell Taylor points out.

"We conduct bimonthly mini-classes with all consumer representatives," he says. "They take appliances apart and put them back together again. They're kept abreast of modifications and new features and, of course, taught about new products and services as they are introduced. They're more, much more than telephone operators," he concluded.

An integral part of the basic training program is structured role playing with a total of sixteen hours being devoted to identifying caller personalities and learning how to respond to the identified personalities. GE has identified seven basic caller personalities and has established a response personality for each.

CHANGING PERSONALITY

Caller Personality	Response Personality
1. Direct/Natural	Efficient, confident and pleasantly professional.
2. Pleasant/Outgoing	Equally pleasant, outgoing, friendly, exchanging a bit of small talk.
3. Insecure/Anxious	Nurturing parent, reassuring, generating a sense of well-being.
4. Confused/Uncertain	Patient, caring, clarifying.
5. Angry/Belligerent	Empathic listening, responding positive with understanding and follow through with professional action.
6. Emergency/Panic	An equal sense of urgency in dialog and in proposing action.
7. Skeptical/Cynical	Reassuring, knowledgeable response with professional expertise.

When role-playing session training is completed, consumer representatives are capable of identifying caller personalities a few seconds into the conversation. The ease with which representatives handle calls must be seen and heard to be believed.

REPRESENTATIVE ATTITUDES

Based on the theory that the best way to learn how people feel about themselves is to ask them, we did just that.

"The one thing we all seem to share in common," Kathy Beck, a fine arts graduate and former GE kitchen designer, said in referring to the family of representatives, "is a high degree of empathy. We sincerely try to help people who call here," she said. "Sometimes callers are frustrated or angry. When we listen and respond, it makes a difference to them. And that's a very satisfying feeling for us."

We chatted with Alice Semonin over lunch in the Center's lunchroom, which was equipped with the latest GE microwaves, toasters, coffeemakers, and refrigerators. Alice is pert, attractive, and outgoing. A graduate of the University of Georgia where she majored in marketing, she came to The GE Answer Center™ after gaining experience as a customer service person with Hertz.

"What is your position, Alice?" "I'm a supervisor." (The Center has one supervisor for each fifteen people.) "Alice, don't you and your people experience 'burn out' from spending eight hours a day on the phone, day after day?" "I'm a self-motivator. We all are. I motivate myself at the start of each day, and I never take my frustrations home with me."

"Alice, several times today we've heard all of you referred to as a 'family.' Are you really a close group?" "Yes, we are. We help each other out all the time. And we have lots of fun together. Many of us are close friends socially."

"Finally, Alice, how do you handle the occasional caller who is really nasty?" "Well, if the person swears we make clear at the outset that we don't talk to people who swear. The best way to handle a belligerent person is to be a good listener ... to have plenty of empathy. The key is to control the conversation in a polite, positive way."

Some calls are both fun and rewarding. Richard Andersen, a technical specialist at the Center, told the story of a call from a frantic customer whose kitten had gotten caught under her dryer.

"She said she could see the kitten's leg," said Andersen. "So for about a half-hour I explained to her how to take the dryer apart, while she yelled the instructions across the room to her son. When they freed the kitten, she asked me to hold on for a minute. The next thing I heard was a meow. 'My kitten just wanted to say thank you,' the lady said." High touch!

Kathy, Alice, Richard, all of them—they speak with one voice. They're young—the consumer representatives have an average age of 29. They're well educated—the representatives average 14.5 years of education.

They are all outgoing. The technical specialists, as one would expect, are slightly older with a more technical education and background.

ENVIRONMENT AND MOTIVATION

Not enough can be said about the environment in which the staff functions each day—nor the motivation to excellence.

The atmosphere is Williamsburg, both outside and inside. Plenty of natural and artificial light. The workstations are roomy, well-organized, neat, quiet, and private.

With thousands of calls flowing into the Center each weekday, one would expect constant bedlam. Quite the opposite: Phones don't ring— a red light signals a call on the representative's console. Each representative wears a combination earphone and mouthpiece and speaks to the caller in a normal conversational tone. The accoustics are so effective that no voices are heard in The GE Answer Center™, even though over 100 conversations might be in progress at any one time.

The Center's sophisticated telephone system has an automatic distributor for rapid circulation of calls. All representatives answer by giving their own names. (It's all part of Powell Taylor's "talking to real people" dictum.) The system is geared so that generally no caller need wait for over thirty seconds, if at all.

The system's computer also automatically issues a printout of the status of twenty separate functions at hourly intervals, functions such as number of calls offered to the system, number of calls delayed, average speed of answers, and so on. Printouts allow GE to determine peak periods and project staffing needs accordingly. By tracking history, the Center knows, for example, what extra influx of calls to expect each time a TV commercial appears—by hour, by time of day or night.

"The home is great. The equipment is superb, state-of-the-art. But how do you motivate your people?" Powell Taylor was asked. "We employ four major elements," he replied.

The "family" spirit carries right to the work station.

"1. Recognition of achievements

2. Participation in the Center's activities

3. Giving of responsibilities

4. Opportunities for advancement"

A variety of activities make these elements come alive. There is a steady flow of contests—simple, fun contests. A recent contest, for example, awarded a prize to the representative who handled call number 2,000,000. Excitement was at fever pitch the day the call came to Diane Rinehardt.

When Powell Taylor appears on a TV talk show, chances are that one of his representatives will also be on the show. When brochures are prepared, a real, live Answer Center representative appears in the brochure. When ads and TV commercials are created, Center people are central to them. When press interviews are conducted, Powell Taylor insists that his people be part of the interview. It's recognition and involvement of the highest order.

And, not unlike any polite family member, representatives play host to visitors in their own special way. When a visitor comes by—there are many - the name of the visitor appears on the bottom of the screen of each representative. As the visitor passes stations, the visitor is greeted with smiles and a pleasant "Good morning, Mr. _____." Nice touch.

Consistent with the family spirit, birthdays—there's one or more almost every day—are cause for celebration. "Today is Kathy's birthday. Have some cake with her" appears on the bottom of every video screen. Kathy's station is appropriately adorned with balloons and a birthday poster. And there's a big birthday cake on her desk for all to share. (Sharing: It's part of the motivation process.)

One of the favorite activities at the Center is the sharing of complimentary letters received by the thousands each year. Powell Taylor shares such letters with the individual representatives about whom callers write. He mounts especially interesting letters on a bulletin board for all to see. (Exhibits 2.3 and 2.4 are typical.)

Each consumer representative is accorded special recognition on his or her birthday.

9/11/83

Dear Mr. Taylor,

SEP 15 1983

G.E. ANSWER CENTER

"Thank You" for your help line in the Long Island Newsday. What a great idea!!

Your operator was most helpful in solving a hot oven problem, & most courteous. You & she saved me a repair /call visit & it took my husband about 5 minutes to follow the instructions we were given.

Our house has all G.E. major appliances (over 20 years) as well as small ones — & we will continue to use G.E.

Thank you once again

Most sincerely

Mrs J Joy Berg

221 Aldware Ave.

Island Park, N.Y. 11558

Exhibit 2.3. Reproduction of a "Thank you" letter from a satisfied customer.

August 25, 1983

Mr. John Cappadona
42 Mabro Drive
Denville, N.J. 07834

Mr. Powell Taylor
GENERAL ELECTRIC ANSWER CENTER
9500 Williamsburg Park
Louisville, Ky. 40222

Dear Mr. Taylor,

During the week of August 22, 1983 I called the Answer Center on several occasions
for advice on repairing my G.E. clothes washer. It was my first experience with
your group, and I must tell you, sir, that I was very impressed with the expertise
of the technical staff in correctly diagnosing the problem and helping me work
through the repair procedures.

Equally important, was the courteousness, patience and concern they displayed in
helping a frustrated "do-it-yourselfer" solve the problem in the face of mounting
laundry, and a skeptical wife tapping her foot!

Please express my sincere thanks and appreciation to Messrs. Perks, Simpson,
Cunningham and Anderson for their efforts.

I purchased G.E. products initially because of quality and reliability, and have
always been very satisfied. Your willingness now to offer technical advice (which,
of course, saved me money on a service call) has reinforced my belief that G.E. is
dedicated to serving its customers.

You can be sure I will continue to purchase G.E. products in the future and
recommend them to my friends.

Sincerely,

John Cappadona

P.S. Even the phone call was free! Thanks again.

JC:jct

Exhibit 2.4. Reproduction of another "Thank you" letter from a satisfied
customer.

Representatives share in roundtable discussions, demonstrations,
and retraining. They likewise participate in tours, shows, and meetings.
Films and information meetings are regular fare. Opinion surveys are
shared by all. It's high touch, starting on the inside and reaching to the
outside.

PROOF OF PERFORMANCE

"Now for a really tough question, Powell. How do you know that the millions of dollars spent in building and maintaining The GE Answer Center have been worth it?" He didn't say it, but Powell Taylor looked like a fellow who was thinking to himself "I thought they would never ask!"

"Surveys have shown that 95 percent of the callers to the Center express satisfaction with the service," he said. "Our research brought expressions from consumers showing that they feel GE is with them 24 hours a day, 7 days a week, including holidays. They are more likely to buy a GE product," Powell said, "because they know that at three o'clock in the morning if they have a problem with their furnace or refrigerator, they'll have help. As a matter of fact, many consumers tell us they have bought or will buy GE products because of The Answer Center.

"More than 99 percent of surveyed dealers—GE has 20,000 consumer product dealers and agents—regard The GE Answer Center™ to be a 'super idea,'" Powell continued. "That's because it helps take the monkey off their backs by referring any questions to GE. And they love the way GE refers sales leads to them," he concluded.

PROMOTING THE GE ANSWER CENTER

GE has the people, the training facility, the answers—500,000 of them—but the consumer still has to know about The GE Answer Center™. And GE makes sure the consumer does know ... in every conceivable way. We spoke earlier about press interviews and talk shows. But the word doesn't start there. It starts with the word to GE's 20,000 dealers (see Exhibit 2.5) and carries through in their print (see Exhibit 2.6) and broadcast (see Exhibit 2.7)—even in their annual report to stockholders.

All product literature, whatever the line, carries the legend "Your Direct Line to General Electric ... The GE Answer Center™ 800.626.2000." And the word about the Center carries through to all use and care booklets consumers get with GE products. But GE doesn't even stop there: The toll free number—800.626.2000—appears on most products purchased. So GE is never more than a phone call away.

THE ANSWER TO ANSWER CENTER SUCCESS

"Could you summarize the reasons for the success of The GE Answer Center?" was our next to last question. "It starts with commit-

The GE Answer Center 800.626.2000

9500 Williamsburg Plaza   Louisville, Kentucky 40222

September 24, 1981

Greetings,

Enclosed you will find the GE Answer Center merchandising kit...a total
package specifically designed to enhance brand image (to increase sales)
and relieve you of answering numerous customers' questions regarding GE
consumer products and services.

Each kit contains . . .

A Counter Card

The Counter Card boldly draws attention to our new Answer Center service.
Display it in a prominent, high traffic area. The Counter Card pocket
holds attractive brochures which explain the benefits of the Answer
Center to your customers. The Counter Card also holds a pad of self-
adhesive labels listing the Answer Center's toll-free number. Urge your
customers to take one of each.

A Program Brochure

This brochure explains why the GE Answer Center was developed, how it
operates, and how it can work for you. Inside the back flap you'll
find an example of the consumer brochure, 4-color ad reprints being
placed in your area, media schedules, and repro art slugs you can use
in your own retail advertising to promote the GE Answer Center.

In the kit you'll also find an additional supply of consumer brochures
and labels to keep your counter card fully stocked.

I urge you to take a few minutes to read through the program brochure.
Then assemble and display your Counter Card and begin promoting the
GE Answer Center in your advertising. By tying-in with us, we'll
answer your questions for you - so you can concentrate on selling.

Good luck.

Regards,

Powell Taylor

N. P. TAYLOR
Manager
GE Answer Center

Encl.

GENERAL
ELECTRIC

Exhibit 2.5. Reproduction of a letter sent to 20,000 GE dealers explaining
the advantages to them of The GE Answer Center.™

LIP
SERVICE.

Exhibit 2.6. A two-page GE magazine ad directed to consumers, explaining the advantages of using The GE Answer Center.™

GE SERVICE.

Ever get the feeling when you buy an appliance that all the service you were promised was nothing more than lip service?

Well, at General Electric we've built an entire program around service. All *kinds* of service. To help you *before, during* and *after* you buy.

GE: OPEN FOR QUESTIONS 24 HOURS A DAY.

Imagine picking up your phone, day or night, and getting an answer to any question you have about a GE consumer product. That's the GE Answer Center.™ Call toll-free 800-626-2000. It's that easy.

STRONG PRODUCTS MEAN LONG WARRANTIES.

The longer the warranty, the better. That's why GE gives you a full 10-year warranty on the PermaTuf®tubs in our dishwashers. A full 2-year warranty on most GE telephones. An exclusive, full 2-year warranty on

electric skillets. And a limited 1-year warranty on GE Command Performance™ television products.

TWO KINDS OF HELP.

Should anything go wrong with a GE product, you'll have access to a nationwide network of factory-trained technicians.

And for many of our major appliances, if you'd rather fix it yourself, there's our Quick Fix™ system. Complete with repair manuals and easy-to-install parts.

GE GIVES YOU THE CREDIT YOU DESERVE.

We may even be able to help you finance your major appliance purchase. With fast, convenient credit at modest rates. So that buying a GE appliance will be a simple, easy experience.

NO ONE HELPS YOU LIKE GE.

You already know the frustration of lip service. Now try GE service. There's no other service like it.

WE BRING GOOD THINGS TO LIFE.

Exhibit 2.6 continued.

39

BBDO
Batten, Barton, Durstine & Osborn, Inc.

Client: GENERAL ELECTRIC   Time: 60 SECONDS

Product: GE SERVICES   Title: "SERVICE"   Comml. No: GECS-3026

(SFX: STREET SOUNDS)
DELIVERYMAN: Here you are!
HUSBAND: Thanks, guys!

WIFE: Oh, we forgot to ask about the...
HUSBAND: Right! I'll get him back before he gets back in the truck.

AVO: Ever get the feeling when you buy something that once you get it home...

You're out on your own?

Well, it's a lot different with GE. We're always there to help.

OPERATOR: Hello, GE Answer Center, may I help you? AVO: With an Answer Center to answer your questions 24 hours a day.

MAN: Oh? Put that one in input and that one in output.

AVO: With Servicemen who show up at your convenience.
WOMAN: Sorry we're late.

AVO: Or if you'd like to fix it yourself, there's the GE Quick Fix System.

GIRL: Simply, tighten screw and you're finished.

AVO: And with GE financing, you may be able to get that kitchen you've wanted for years...practically overnight.

With GE you never feel alone.
SINGERS: GE, we bring good things to life.

Exhibit 2.7. GE TV commercial explaining the availability of the GE Answer System.

ment," Powell said, "from the top of the organization right down through the ranks. Consumers are sometimes startled when Jack Welch, our chairman, calls them personally about a letter they wrote. Our directors call the Center often," he added. "And I can't put too much emphasis on screening, training, facilities, recognition, participation, and family spirit," he concluded.

EMULATION POSSIBILITIES

Our last question was "the $64 question." "Considering that you are a Fortune 500 company—huge—would you say that the 'little fellow' can emulate what you have done?"

"It depends," said Powell, "upon commitment and product complexity. A toe-in-the-water approach never works. Many have tried a half-hearted approach and failed. Of course, few companies are as complex as ours with 120 product lines and 8,500 models. For most firms, therefore, the database need not be anywhere as large as ours.

"As a matter of fact, a regional package goods company, for example, could effectively set up an answer center with their database being a notebook containing answers to every conceivable question. In reality, the answer to 'Can I mix your pudding with a cake mix?' is just as important to a homemaker as 'How do I hook up your VCR?' to an electronic buff," Powell Taylor concluded.

After we left, we couldn't wait to call The GE Answer Center™: "Could you please tell us the name of the melody you are using in your GE lighting commercial and who composed it?" "Certainly. The name of the melody is 'Canon.' It was composed by Johann Pachelbel, who lived from 1653 to 1703. It is performed by the Stuttgart Chamber Orchestra and is available on records by London." "Thank you, Betty." "You're welcome."

The GE Answer Center™. It works!

CHAPTER 3

The AT&T National Sales Center

Most people think of "Everything's Up to Date in Kansas City" as a parody from the musical *Oklahoma*. But for the citizens of this surprising city, the refrain is melodic reality.

They point with pride to their magnificent Country Club Plaza, the prototype of upscale shopping centers around the world. They are proud of their Kansas City Symphony, their Lyric Opera, their Nelson-Atkins Museum of Art, and their Missouri Repertory Theatre.

The park system is unrivaled by any American city: over 125 parks with more fountains than any city outside Europe and the ultra-modern twin stadia in the Truman Memorial Sports Complex that serves as separate homes for their professional baseball and football teams. The "Cow Town" image of the Pendergast era is a thing of the past.

What is little known about Kansas City—even by long-time residents—is that possibly the most up-to-date state-of-the-art Telemarketing Center in all the world is a three-minute walk from Crown Center, the showcase of Hallmark Cards. Housed within two stories of this modern office building at 2301 Main Street is the AT&T National Sales Center.

THE GENESIS OF THE CENTER

"We're here to see the manager of your Center—Mr. Mike Closz."
"Yes, he's expecting you. Won't you have a seat, please."

43

"Mike, as you know, we're writing a book on Telemarketing. And from what we know of your Center and its growth, we feel you have a great deal to give to the readers of our book." "We'll be glad to share whatever we have," Mike Closz said. "But first let me have two of my associates join us: Ed Sellers, our sales manager, and Susan Bryant, our account executive for major markets."

You've got to like Ed Sellers right off. Exuberant. Dedicated. A motivator. And Susan Bryant strikes you as the epitome of an M.B.A. who has moved up steadily through the ranks. Friendly. Knowledgeable. And customer-oriented.

After reiterating our mission, Mike Closz suggested that we proceed to their presentation room, a room replete with the most up-to-date audiovisual equipment. "First we want to show you the history of growth of Telemarketing at AT&T," Mike said.

"The reason for starting at this point," he continued, "is that we consider our Center to be a testing arena where we can prove and refine techniques. We pass on our proved techniques to customers and would-be customers." For the next twelve minutes, we were immersed

Mike Closz, center manager, reviewing Telemarketing basics with his associates Ed Sellers and Susan Bryant.

in the sights and sounds of a fascinating audiovisual presentation that detailed the genesis of the AT&T Telemarketing Center. The audio portion tells the story.

> The NSC story ... a story about people combining marketing strategies with telecommunications and information technology to create an innovative marketing system: *Telemarketing*. For over a *decade* AT&T has been experimenting and perfecting Telemarketing ... to meet the needs of the corporation in a rapidly-changing economic environment.

> This is that story. In the early 1970s, AT&T responded to a negative economic climate by introducing national account management as the centerpiece of its marketing communications mix. These national account teams were supported by other marketing communication methods—trade shows, executive communication and demonstration centers, direct mail and media advertising.

> This marketing mix served as a revenue pipeline, to and from our customers. Its cornerstone was face to face selling. And it worked—we were successfully meeting our revenue goals.

> But then—the mid-seventies—more external pressures: energy, competition, recession, inflation. The cost of doing business skyrockets ... and hits all forms of personal selling the hardest.

> These external pressures were beginning to constrict the revenue flow. Something had to be done to maintain the flow...to supplement our current marketing mix. That something was Telemarketing.

> The first step in our attempt to increase revenue was to examine our marketplace. We were confronted with a textbook marketing case—20% of our customers provided 80% of our revenue. That meant that 80% of our customer base was left virtually unmanaged—never receiving a face to face visit.

> The goal of our Telemarketing program—to access the enormous untapped revenue potential in this market segment. To increase our opportunities to sell network services, we decided to target "WATS" to generate new leads for our field sales force. 800 numbers were placed in our advertising. A small group was organized to take the calls and forward the leads to the field for follow-up.

> The initial response was impressive.

> To measure the performance of our promotions, a manual tracking system was created. A timeshare firm was contracted to process the data. We soon discovered that our television and radio campaigns were not particularly effective for a product of this complexity. Our

direct mail programs, coupled with print advertising in a select group of publications, proved the most successful.

The ability to measure the performance of these promotions enabled us to continually refine, modify, and thus improve our advertising effectiveness. In just a few months, we had dramatically increased the number of leads—while drastically decreasing their cost. By year's end, this pilot program had netted another result that was even more important—in fact, it was spectacular—our first experience with Telemarketing had increased national sales by $14 million. Clearly, we were on the threshold of some new opportunities.

It wasn't long before all this success at sales lead generation had an interesting side effect. The quantity of new leads was impressive— so impressive that the sales force had no effective way of handling, or even qualifying, all of these new potential accounts. The problem was one of quantity versus quality. The next step in the evolution of this Telemarketing program would be to confront this problem.

In 1977, based on the success of our pilot program, the first National Sales Center was built—and with it, a new set of objectives. The NSC would move from simple *sales lead generation*—up to an effective method of *sales lead qualification.*

The corporate commitment was made to meet this more complex goal. The sophistication of the database was increased. Highly educated, qualified personnel were hired and trained in consultative selling techniques. By entering the information they gathered into the database, customer profiles were built—size, gross, industry, wholesale, retail, current telecommunication services and so on ... the more complete the database—the more efficient the qualification process became.

The quantity of calls that came in dictated that we increase the sales staff, gradually, from 6 to 21. A state-of-the-art automatic call distribution system was installed to distribute the calls evenly among available personnel, insuring prompt, professional service.

With these elements in place, the Center became more effective. By 1978, the NSC had netted more impressive results—the tracking and measurement of our advertising allowed us to cut our promotional expenses in half, increasing our revenue to expense ratio by 16% and best of all, the sales lead qualification process was working. The national closing ratio on sales visits is one in ten. In one year, our Telemarketing program brought our sales force a closing ratio of better than *6.5 in 10.*

But there was another result that was even more important: data. Information that could be used for more than just servicing our

Individual stations of AT&T consultants.

customers. In the course of refining and improving our techniques we had built a database that could be used for market research— information that would help us devise the next step in the evolution of our Telemarketing strategy. The research revealed that a large percentage of the customers who called were still too small to qualify for a sales visit—yet they shared similar needs that could be solved by telecommunications products and services. A cost effective method was needed to sell this large group of marginal accounts. Again that method was Telemarketing.

The NSC now had the confidence and skill to move up from its role in sales support to order processing. New objectives with specific response, sales and expense goals were set.

The NSC would now use consultative selling techniques to actually sell a broader range of products and services to solve customer problems. And, most important, they would handle as many calls as possible. All by phone—without ever involving the field sales force. To achieve this goal, the sales staff was increased to 30. Salary and education levels rose (40% now have graduate degrees). Training was intensified to include five full weeks of classroom sessions. The data system was expanded to accommodate order entry functions. Customer files were made more complete. The database would continue to measure the performance of our promotions—but now it would measure the performance of our people as well.

With these changes in place the NSC was off and running again—learning, changing and refining its methods … capable of handling over 1,000 calls per day.

Media buys were staggered to control incoming calling volume—thus avoiding the overload or under utilization of personnel. The large staff required to handle incoming volume during peak hours was also available for a host of outbound programs … cold calls, follow ups, sales validations, new program testing and coupon responses, were all made when incoming volume was low—thus evening out productivity.

Couponing reinforced a lot of what we already knew about the power of Telemarketing: although our responses run half coupon, half 800 number, we close twice as many sales on the people who call in. The key? *Timing.* The 800 number allows us to be there, when the customer is most interested.

Since its inception, the NSC has produced spectacular results.

The Center has experienced a 20% annual growth rate, and now handles over 300,000 contacts a year. A full 95% of these calls are managed by the Center. 5% are referred to the field. The NSC now has an earning potential of well over 100 million dollars per year.

You are now sitting in today's NSC: a critical link in AT&T Communications' marketing strategy. Its objectives: to sell and service six million new and existing AT&T customers. Its functions: full account management, order processing, sales support and customer service—the full range of Telemarketing applications.

The corporate commitment has been strengthened … our relationship with the field has been enhanced … and the selection and training process has been fine-tuned enabling our sales consultants to sell an even broader range of products and services to a wider variety of customers. Like its predecessors, today's NSC is built on sound management methods. Objectives are set … programs to meet those objectives are implemented … measured … and finally, modified to better meet those—or new objectives. A continuing process that allows us to combine the right people and the right Telemarketing applications with the right Center management techniques.

Today's NSC works. It works because it is based on a marketing system that offers the vital elements of two way, personal communications—a flexible marketing system that produces real time measurable results. Accurate market research that can be used to test, grow, change, and improve that system ... because Telemarketing is a system that is evolutionary.

And finally—the NSC works because Telemarketing is a cost effective enhancement, replacement and/or addition to any marketing mix ... because the customer is ready for it ... the economic climate requires it ... and because the future demands it.

THE AT&T NETWORK CONSULTANTS

As the audio-visual presentation concluded, the panel of one long wall moved in *Star Wars* fashion into a recess, revealing a panoramic view of the Sales Center in action. Before us were the AT&T Network Consultants—the heartbeat of the Center.

Dressed for face-to-face contact—á la the GE Answer Center—each was in voice-to-voice communication with either a prospect or customer. Each workstation was tantamount to a Telemarketing satellite, complete with CRT, telephone, and manuals.

"May we meet one of your network consultants?" we asked. "Certainly. I think you'd really enjoy meeting one of the younger members of our staff—Chris Launius." "Great."

We met privately with Chris. And the dialogue that ensued revealed a young man thoroughly schooled in the MBO concept—his career objectives clearly established. His poise was remarkable for one who had not yet passed his twenty-third year.

"How long have you been at the National Sales Center, Chris?" "Eleven months." "What is your educational background?" "I graduated from Mid-America Nazarene College with a double major in Public Relations and Business. I have an M.B.A. in PR."

"Did you have any opportunity to practice what you learned while at college?"

"Yes—I was a radio and TV sports announcer and writer during my college days."

"Well, how did you happen to get a position at the AT&T National Sales Center?"

"I sent out a number of resumes. AT&T responded, interviewed me, and offered me a position."

"What type of training were you given here at the Sales Center?" "I had five weeks of classroom training that included basic selling skills, knowledge of equipment, and role playing. Then I was monitored for an additional five weeks with supervisors reviewing calls with me, pointing out how I could best improve my techniques."

"What do you like most about your position, Chris?" "The thing I like best about my position is that I get immediate feedback from my efforts and immediate recognition from my peers and supervisors."

"But it's not all gratification?" "Certainly not. I get frustrated with my own performance. And I still experience fear of failure. I often get mentally fatigued. I still tend to take my job home with me. Working out every night helps to clear my mind."

"Tell us about your work day, Chris." "Well, I come in at 7:45 A.M. I spend about six hours a day on the phone. I have anywhere from 35 to 45 phone conversations a day. The real payoff is that I close over 50% of my prospects on the first call."

"Even with this high closure rate, you must have a large number of prospects whom you consider to be worthy of follow-up calls." "Yes—I have anywhere from 100 to 170 qualified prospects in queue for followup at any one time. My CRT reveals these for me automatically." (See Exhibit 3.1.)

"Chris—what method do you use to qualify prospects?" "Well, as you know, we're schooled in consultative selling techniques. There are five things I want to learn to qualify a prospect quickly: (1) Am I talking to the decision maker, or a person who influences the decision maker?

Chris Launius, consultant, in the process of making a sale.

```
                        RESPONSE INFORMATION REPORT

RESPONSE NUMBER: DN2394    SPEC. INITIALS: JCB      HOW RECD: WATS
DATE:  5/27/83             TIME:  5:21              REFERRED TO: LOS

RESPOND TO:                            CALLER INFORMATION:
NAME    : MR. ██████████████
TITLE   : PRESIDENT
COMPANY: ████████████████████
ADDRESS: ███████████████████
CITY    : LOS ANGELES
STATE   : CA           ZIP CODE: 90045
PHONE   : 213-████████  P.S.T.              213-██████████


PROGRAM: JUNE TELEMKTG.   H29    '83
MEDIA   : INC
SCOPE OF BUSINESS: NATIONAL
SIC     : 7300-BUSINESS SERVICE INCLUDING DATA PRO
SALES POTENTIAL   : MEDIUM
INITIAL ACTION    : FOR ESSC SALES CONTACT
DECISION MAKER    : YES         SEX: MALE
MM CODE: 243-ENERGY AND RESOURCE UTILITIES


BROCHURE DESCRIP : EXPAND BUS. BY OPEN NEW ACCTS  DATE MAILED: 10/06/83
QUANTITY BROCHURES REQUESTED:  1
BROCHURE DESCRIP : PROFESSIONAL TELMKTG EDUCATIO  DATE MAILED:  7/01/83
QUANTITY BROCHURES REQUESTED:  1
BROCHURE DESCRIP : CUSTOMER TRAINING MATERIALS    DATE MAILED:  1/17/84
QUANTITY BROCHURES REQUESTED:  1
BROCHURE DESCRIP : TELEMARKETING PILOT            DATE MAILED:  1/17/84
QUANTITY BROCHURES REQUESTED:  1
BROCHURE DESCRIP : WHOLESALER GUIDE TO INSIDE SL  DATE MAILED:  6/09/83
QUANTITY BROCHURES REQUESTED:  1

    REMARKS:
COMPUTER COMPANY, STRONG INTEREST IN TM.  ARE RELOCATING, WANT INFO ON
TM STATION ENVIRONMENT.  ARE CONDUCTING OUTGOING ONA PROGRAM (12 WATS
LINES) ARE STARTING DM CAMPAIGN.  HAVE 12 PEOPLE ON PHONES, ONLY 2 800
LINES.  FUP TO REVIEW WHOLESALE GUIDE AND DM PROGRAM, 800 LINE CONFIG.,
ETC.



INTEREST: 21 - TELEMARKETING
QUALIFYING QUESTIONS:
  1.COUNTING YOUR LOCATION,TOTAL LOCATIONS IN YOUR CO?: 1
  2.HOW MANY PEOPLE ARE EMPLOYED AT YOUR LOCATION?    : 15-24
  3.WHAT WAS LAST YEARS SALES VOLUME?                 : CUST REFUSED
  4.YOUR COMPANY'S PRIMARY USE OF LD TELEPHONE?       : SALES
  5.ARE YOU PRESENTLY USING ANY OF THESE SERVICES?    : 800/WATS INTER
  6.DO YOU HAVE ANY PLANS FOR EXPANSION?              : YES-DEFINITE
  7.WHAT KIND OF ADVERTISING/PROMOTION DO YOU USE?    : DIRECT MAIL


FOLLOW-UP INFORMATION
SPECIALIST  : RLL                CONTACT DATE:  2/23/84
FINAL ACTION: FOLLOW UP
SCHEDULED FOLLOW-UP DATE    :  2/13/84
```

Exhibit 3.1. CRT printout of follow-up information for Network Consultant.

(2) Does the firm have expansion plans? (3) Can they afford the equipment and service that would be required? (4) Does the prospect truly see the need? (5) Would they spend the money? If answers to key questions are negative, the conversation is concluded quickly," said Chris Launius.

"You've had your good days and your bad days, we're sure. What has been your greatest day at the Center?" This brought a broad smile across Chris' face. "My greatest day," he said, "was recently when I completed a $2.2 million sale by telephone—the largest ever. Adding this to my normal production, I accounted for $3 million in a four-month period."

"Chris, you've told us that you are an MBO person. How are you applying management by objective to your present and future career goals?" "Well, I work against a quota and I am evaluated each month and quarter, as all consultants are. I like that.

"As to career goals, I want to mature to the point that I will be managing sales. And further, I want to apply my acquired skills in public relations."

"Well then, Chris, can we conclude that your eleven-month stint at the AT&T National Sales Center has been a good learning experience?" "I feel that I have learned more in this short period than in all my graduate-school experience. I've 'met' all types of people and have learned the intricacies of all sizes of businesses," he said.

The interview completed, this intense young man returned to his workstation to live his goals of qualifying prospects, closing better than one out of two qualified prospects on the first call and following up on prospects who were not closed on previous calls. What was so remarkable about this interview was that we came to realize that there were some 65 additional Network Consultants on the premises, all cut pretty much out of the same piece of cloth!

SERVING WOULD-BE TELEMARKETERS

Returning to Ed Sellers, the dynamic sales manager, we said, "We've met firsthand the prototype of an AT&T Network Consultant. But now we'd like to know how the Center serves would-be Telemarketers, particularly national accounts."

"Glad you asked," Ed said. "It's part of our mission to work with our Account Executives evaluating the Telemarketing potential of the national companies they serve, and to pass on our knowledge and expertise, where applicable. Over a given twelve-month period, we make over 200 sales demonstrations for would-be Telemarketers right here at the Center.

"These presentations are tailored to the specific needs of each. Recommendations could include one application or a combination of applications, including order taking, customer service, sales lead qualification, marginal account management, consultative selling, or full account management," Ed concluded.

One didn't have to spend many more hours at the National Sales Center to observe that *everyone* is motivated. It was obvious that this was no accident. We smelled a key to success. And a one-hour meeting with Michael Closz, Director of the Center, confirmed it.

If ever a background of a person fit a position, this one seemed to be the perfect fit. In June 1970, Michael Closz was a Captain-Company Commander in the United States Marine Corps. In June 1972, he was awarded a Bachelor of Arts Degree at Michigan State University; in June 1973, a Bachelor of Science Degree; and in June 1975, a Masters Degree in Business Administration.

His career path with AT&T started the same year—1975—when he was made Operations Manager, AT&T Long Lines, Springfield, Illinois. Rapid promotions followed: sales manager, national account manager, director human resources, district operations manager. And in January 1983, Michael Closz was made director of the AT&T National Sales Center in Kansas City, Missouri. A fast track, as the saying goes.

During the first year, Michael Closz' accomplishments were heralded in a front-page story in the October 27, 1983, issue of the *Wall Street Journal* in which Closz predicted he would be able to exceed his 1983 revenue objective of $70 million by 50%. (He reached the prediction of $104 million.) And in telling the story to the *Journal*, this 6'2" ex-Marine at a trim 195 pounds gave due credit to his nine sales managers, sixty-five network consultants, and thirty-five support personnel.

"Mike—this Center has the sweet smell of success. Motivation seems to be the key. Can you give us motivational concepts that you believe can be applied by others?" "Not all situations are identical, of course. But I'll be glad to share the concepts we apply at the Center," he said. What follows is a distillation of the Center's ongoing motivational program.

MOTIVATIONAL HIERARCHY

The motivational program is structured as a hierarchy of three phases: (1) tactical or short-term motivation, (2) strategic or intermediate motivation, and (3) long-term motivation.

Tactical motivation is directed at meeting overall revenue objectives from day to day. Strategic or intermediate motivation is applied to consultants in the development of their Telemarketing and corporate skills and, at the same time, to suppress burnout, boredom, and anxiety. The objective of long-term motivation is to maintain a high degree of expectation for future career opportunities and advancement.

Phase One: Tactical or Short-Term Motivation

Tactics for Short-Term Motivation

Two major tactics are involved in day-to-day motivations: (1) incentives, and (2) frequent recognition. Addressing incentives as a tactic, Mike Closz gave three reasons why incentive plans often fail.

1. The lesser achievers often view the award as unachievable.
2. There is a tendency on the part of many telephone specialists to believe that there is an opportunity for distortion, or dishonest attainment of prizes.
3. The reward is often inconsistent with the objective. (An example of inconsistency would be where the objective was *accurate qualification of prospects*, but the incentive was based upon the number of leads referred to the field *regardless of qualification*.)

"The objective of any incentive plan," Closz cautioned, "is to develop work habits and standards that will continue to benefit the Telemarketing Center long after a prize has been awarded."

Applying Plan to Objective

We asked Mike Closz to give us a couple of examples of the proper application of incentives to objectives. The first example follows.

Objective. To increase the sales of the AT&T Calling Card. (It should be noted that consultants receive no individual dollar credit for the sale of cards.)

Incentive. The group with the most cards sold was to be treated to a recognition breakfast. (On the surface, this doesn't sound like much of an incentive.)

Procedure. Four groups were set up: Two groups were offered the incentive, two were not.

Results. The two groups participating in the contest sold 2,200 cards by the end of the quarter; the two groups not participating totaled only 129 cards for the quarter. The incentive plan resulted in an additional revenue of $92,400—all for the cost of a breakfast!

Continuing benefits. To maintain productivity for the AT&T Calling Card program after the contest, sales managers held each Network Consultant accountable for the number of cards sold. And to dramatize the continuing importance of the program, a chart was posted at the sales group's board with daily tracking of cards sold. Proof of success is the fact that the number of cards sold after the contest equalled those sold during the contest period.

The second example applies to a different tactic—team motivation.

Objective. To motivate the largest possible number of Telemarketing specialists.

The rationale. Individuals who usually are not motivated by incentive programs often exert extra effort toward group success. Therefore, if group motivation is applied, productivity will be increased by the largest number.

Procedure. The lowest performing group of four sales groups was singled out for a team motivation contest. Figures showed that this group was drastically short of the contact objectives expected of them. And experience showed that most members of this group viewed other contests as unattainable individually since their contact level was far behind their co-workers.

The goal. A goal was set for the team as a whole. The individuals in this group became accountable to each other. What occurred was that members devised an intragroup tracking system and gave encouragement and assistance to any member who appeared to fall behind.

Incentive. Team incentives rather than individual incentives were applied to this group. And the reward system was based more on personal recognition than on individual prizes.

Results. The sales team showed continuing improvement from month-to-month. From a low of 5,315 contacts the first month, they went to 6,293 the second month and 7,231 the third month. The team no longer resided in last place.

Recapping the components of a successful incentive plan, Mike Closz identified three musts: (1) Develop plans that encourage work habits that continue; (2) use plans that are cohesive with the goals of the Telemarketing Center; (3) develop plans that motivate the largest number in the Center.

IMPORTANCE OF RECOGNITION

Part and parcel of every successful incentive plan is recognition, Closz emphasized. Recognition at the AT&T National Sales Center takes many shapes, he pointed out.

1. Monthly reviews are conducted one-on-one with manager and employee, the goal being to communicate positives by praising successes and planning specific actions for improvement.
2. Outstanding achievements are posted regularly for all to see.
3. Verbal recognition is constant. Pats on the back for goals achieved and reassurance of progress are proffered.

Phase Two: Strategic or Intermediate Motivation

We now move to phase two in the motivational hierarchy: development of Telemarketing and corporate skills. "In this phase, we address strategic motivators in three different areas," Closz stated. "One—those that enhance personal development. Two—those that develop skills that improve job performance. Three—motivators for ongoing career pathing that provide direction."

Personal Development

"Personal development reflects how we can influence the individual and the motivation for the job," Closz continued. He then cited examples of job content enrichment.

1. They provide more than average in-depth training about complex products which require technical knowledge and intuitive skills.
2. They target new markets for cold-call programs and train their people to recognize specific needs and objectives for those areas.
3. They consciously break routine as an antidote to monotony. To accomplish this they alternate outbound with inbound calling responsibilities. The objective is continuous movement and change.

Examples of personal development projects done at the Center include employee-developed seminars and workshops that are presented to supervisors and peers, listening skills workshops, individual motivation, and time management programs. Another example is presentations to national account clients who visit the Center. "These projects develop individual organizational skills and initiative," Closz said. "They also provide management with an excellent opportunity to identify leadership potential," he concluded.

Developing Job Performance Skills

"Job performance improves dramatically when strategic motivation is applied to the development of skills," Closz stated. Examples of motivation include:

1. Workshops devoted to selling skills, lead qualification, and listening.

2. The use of a listening post whereby an assigned Network Consultant keeps the sales floor informed about competitive service offerings and makes specific suggestions on how to overcome objections that may arise.

3. Giving sales people the opportunity to create and implement new cold-call programs, targeting markets that they feel offer high potential.

"On the management side," Closz commented, "constant reevaluation of the skill-building training process is required. Training at our Center is evaluated as to its current relation to market design. It is modified, when necessary, to maximize skills relevant to new products and marketing programs."

Career Pathing

Referring specifically to career pathing—a vital area—Closz said, "Career pathing in our Center involves setting goals that meet both corporate and individual objectives, providing continuous feedback to review progress, and exploring opportunities for promotion.

"As an ongoing motivator, career pathing provides direction. This eliminates uncertainty and anxiety about the future.

"The first step toward career pathing is goal setting. What we seek through goal setting is a supportive atmosphere: one in which the employee can grow continuously rather than be subject to authoritarian rule.

"To demonstrate this support, our sales groups participate in both performance and career goal setting. This has increased involvement and a feeling of commitment to established goals. We find that the more employee involvement is allowed, the more we demonstrate our support of our people in their progression toward achievement and promotion.

"Once goals have mutually been set, we make sure each consultant is kept up to date. Feedback and review sessions are conducted monthly and quarterly. The objective of these sessions is to evaluate performance, plan strategy for improvement, and communicate progress toward promotion.

"This process is motivational because of the ongoing attention to employee goals. Our people know where they stand and what they must do to succeed. And success is the most powerful motivator of all.

"Finally," Closz concluded, "career pathing provides management with a tool to assess and evaluate employee strengths and weaknesses.

Through this process, opportunities for growth and promotion can be explored. Employees are able to contemplate how their current performance may be applied to the job opportunities both in Telemarketing and field sales with AT&T."

Phase Three: Long-Term Motivation

The third and final stage of the Center's motivational hierarchy deals specifically with maintaining a high degree of expectation about future career opportunities and advancement.

"Promotion into higher level sales or management is what I consider to be the long-term motivator at the National Sales Center," Mike Closz said. "It is the light at the end of the tunnel, a light kept alive by continuous movement in the Center. Not only do our people hear that excellent performance will lead to bigger and better things, but they actually receive daily, weekly, and monthly reinforcement of this philosophy by observing the process happening to their peers."

The phenomenal growth of the AT&T National Sales Center is living testimony to the soundness of an ongoing motivational hierarchy. It is a model that lends itself to wide adoption.*

KEYS TO SUCCESS

"One final question, Mike: If you could capsulize the keys to Telemarketing success, what would they be?" He summed it up this way:

1. Recruiting against well-established guidelines.
2. Ongoing training to develop and update skills.
3. Continual monitoring of telephone performance.
4. A continuous-loop feedback to Telemarketing specialists.
5. Managers who understand the Telemarketing concept and how it works.
6. Total management commitment.
7. Total understanding of MIS (management information systems) and how they can be utilized.
8. An ongoing motivational hierarchy.

The AT&T National Sales Center: It's a model to follow.

*Note: To meet expanded sales needs, AT&T has now established six regional Telemarketing Centers. The National Sales Center in Kansas City served as the prototype.

CHAPTER 4

Telemarketing in the Advertising Process

"Let Your Fingers Do the Walking." This is, without doubt, one of the most recognized slogans in all the world. It is a symbol for shopping, a symbol for gathering information, a symbol for locating hard-to-find products and services. According to National Yellow Pages Service Association, research covering a twelve-month period showed that 81.5% of adults used the Yellow Pages when considering a purchase.

There are over 6,000 Yellow Pages Directories published. And the headings under which advertising can appear come to a staggering 13,000, of which 4,000 are national. Some $3 billion is spent in Yellow Pages advertising each year.

TELEMARKETING AND YELLOW PAGES ADVERTISING

Today national advertisers buy space in the Yellow Pages in the same manner as they do in magazines or newspapers. They can, with a single space order, get national coverage in as many as 6,000 directories. Or they can get regional ad coverage using just a few directories.

One of the principal applications of Yellow Pages advertising is the use of a trademark heading program for local dealers. KitchenAid **59** automatic dishwashers, for example, is a well-known national brand. A homemaker considering the purchase of a dishwasher turns to the Yellow Pages and there under the heading "Dishwashing Machines" finds a complete listing with phone numbers of the KitchenAid dealers in the area (Exhibit 4.1). KitchenAid runs the same "ad" in all Yellow Pages markets in which they have dealers, simply dropping in the names of the local dealers. Thus, they localize advertising for their national brand.

Use of 800 Number

The 800 number also comes into play in Yellow Pages advertising. Hilton Hotels, using the theme "Now you can make a reservation at any

```
┌─────────────────────────────────────────────┐
│ KITCHENAID APPLIANCES ─────────────────      │
│                                               │
│  DISHWASHERS:        ▐ KitchenAid ▌           │
│  Built-In, Portable,                          │
│  Convertible &                                │
│  Dishwasher-Sinks.   Trash  Compactors,  Food │
│  Waste  Disposers,  Hot-Water  Dispensers. All│
│  built better to last longer.                 │
│                                               │
│           "WHERE TO CALL"                     │
│              DISTRIBUTOR                       │
│  Remco Federal Inc                            │
│      620 Enterprise Dr Oak Brk --------654-2111│
│           AUTHORIZED SALES                     │
│  BRATSCHI PLUMBING CO                          │
│      801 Oak Winetka ------------- 446-1421    │
│  CAHILL JOHN J INC                             │
│      1515 Church Evnstn ----------- 864-5225   │
│  HERROLD KITCHENS & BATHS                      │
│      102 E Dundee Rd Wheeling ------ 537-0250  │
│  KILLIAN V J CO                                │
│      933 Lindn Av Winetka ---------- 446-0908  │
│      1946C Lehigh Glenvw ----------- 724-9045  │
│  KITCHEN & BATH MART                           │
│      3207 Lake Wilmet ------------- 256-7600   │
│  MERGENTHALER G N PLUMBING &                   │
│      HEATING                                   │
│      Sales And Service                         │
│      1148 Depot Glenvw ------------ 724-2004   │
│         AUTHORIZED SALES & SERVICE             │
│  KILLIAN V J CO                                │
│      933 Lindn Av Winetka ---------- 446-0908  │
│      1946C Lehigh Glenvw ----------- 724-9045  │
│  NORTH SHORE REFRIGERATION                     │
│      COMPANY                                   │
│      Golf & Crawford Skokie --------- 677-7100 │
│  RAVINIA PLUMBING-HEATING &                    │
│      APPLIANCE SERV                            │
│      Authorized Sales & Service                │
│      595 Roger Williams Higld Pk ----- 432-5561│
│           AUTHORIZED SERVICE                   │
│  Kitchen Aid Sales & Service                   │
│      620 Enterprise Dr Oak Brk --------986-5540│
└─────────────────────────────────────────────┘
```

Exhibit 4.1.

Hilton in the world, using this toll-free number," was among the first in the hotel industry to see the value of an 800 number in Yellow Pages advertising. Now such advertising is commonplace for hotels. This type of advertising is also widely used by airlines (Exhibit 4.2).

Still another application of the 800 number in Yellow Pages is to provide a dealer locater service. Rather than being given a listing of all dealers in a given city—sometimes the list is extremely long—the Yellow Pages shopper is invited to call an 800 number to get the name, address, and phone number of the nearest dealer.

Sometimes, of course, there are several dealers within a trading area. So the question arises, how does each dealer in each area get a "fair shake"? Wouldn't you know: The computer has figured this out. Through simple programming, the computer selects dealers sequentially in each area so no one dealer is ever favored over another. Even more sophisticated is a computer program that can select the closest dealer simply by punching in the ZIP code of the prospect.

Exhibit 4.2.

Remote Call Forwarding

And now a switch on the use of the 800 number. Research has shown that, knowing an 800 number denotes a distant city, not everyone feels comfortable in making such calls. So a unique solution has been found to overcome that problem.

There's a telephone service called Remote Call Forwarding (RCF) available in more than 400 cities. With RCF, the advertiser gets a local phone number listing in both the Yellow Pages and the white pages. When the local call is placed, the call is automatically forwarded to the city in which the advertiser resides. (The prospect incurs no cost for call forwarding. It is toll-free.)

RCF offers several advantages to the advertisers:

- Local identity and accessibility.

- Calls are forwarded at economical direct dial rates.

- Local identity stimulates calls from local customers.

- An inexpensive way to serve distant locations.

And there are obvious advantages to the consumer:

- The local number can be found easily in the white or Yellow Pages.
- The consumer feels secure in calling a local number.
- There is never a need to call collect.
- The caller reaches headquarters directly.

TELEMARKETING AND TV ADVERTISING

While Yellow Pages serve as a work-a-day medium for Telemarketing opportunities, television stands out as a glamor medium offering exciting opportunities to sell goods and services directly to the consumer wherever the consumer may live. The direct link is the telephone.

Certain advertisers learned early on that they could sell direct to the consumer via TV if their products lent themselves to dramatic demonstrations. A classic in the fledgling days of TV was a blender carrying the trade name Vita-Mix. A pitchman would demonstrate the wonders of this product and the health-giving rewards for ten to fifteen minutes, showing scores of ways to use it, and then urge phone orders: "Operators are waiting for your call."

Well, the TV pitchman is history—thank goodness—as is the ten- to fifteen-minute commercial. Today direct response commercials are prepared with all the finesse and sophistication of extremely expensive commercials one sees on Super Bowl broadcasts. And the selling job is done in no more than 120 seconds.

So let's take a look at some present-day direct response commercials and see how these advertisers use TV to produce millions of inquiries and phone orders annually.

Sales of Services

New York Telephone Company is a major TV advertiser. Among the many services they have offered their customers are information and entertainment services. Such services as Sports Phone, Dial-A-Joke, and Weather.

Exhibit 4.3 shows a thirty-second commerical promoting Sports Phone. In the short span of thirty seconds, the viewer sees fifteen frames with accompanying audio. It is significant to note that the phone number is superimposed over four of the frames with the area codes for a ten-cent call superimposed over two of the frames.

Were these direct-response TV commercials successful? And how! In a twelve-month period New York Telephone Company received millions of incremental phone calls.

Sale of Food Product

"Hello. Is this 1-800-W CASTLE? I'd like you to ship 50 White Castle hamburgers. My address is _____." In Chapter 1, you read that White Castle is getting phone orders from outside their trading area to the tune of 10,000 hamburgers a week just with word-of-mouth advertising.

"If we can get phone orders for 10,000 hamburgers a week just with word-of-mouth advertising," deduced Gail Turley, White Castle ad manager, "think what we can do through the medium of TV advertising." And so White Castle has created a series of very creative TV commercials, each commercial based upon a true life story with nostalgic overtones. Exhibits 4.4 and 4.5 show two of the commercials. In cities

WRK

CLIENT: NEW YORK TELEPHONE CO. TITLE: "FIELD TALK" DATE: 4/8/81
PRODUCT: SPORTS PHONE LENGTH: 30 SECONDS CODE NUMBER: AXSP 0333

1. COACH: (OC) Rocky, (SFX: SNAP)

2. go back out there and run the trap reverse.

3. Green T45R

4. wide out set.

5. Got it?

6. ROCKY: Got it.

7. COACH: Now let's call Sports Phone and find out how the competition's doing.

8. It's 976-1313.

9. ROCKY: Got it!

10. COACH: Now run that play boy.

11. ROCKY: (VO FROM FIELD) 976-1313 Hut!

12. COACH: (SFX: GRUNT) ....that's wrong.... ...that's wrong...

13. ANNCR: (VO) It's no more than a dime in these area codes

14. for all the major scores.

15. On Sports Phone.

Exhibit 4.3.

White Castle
"The Air Force"

DAUGHTER: I miss you, momma. I miss the city, too.

MOMMA: What if we sent you a little bit of your home town.

DAUGHTER: Now, how are you gonna do that?

White Castle hamburgers from back home! You can't get them out here.

My folks sent them!

ROOMMATE: Hey! Johnson's got White Castles!

GANG: White Castles!

DAUGHTER: You know, on my first date we stopped at a White Castle.

SINGERS: WHITE CASTLE HAS THE TASTE SOME PEOPLE WON'T LIVE WITHOUT.

Exhibit 4.4.

White Castle

"Loyalty"

(Anncr VO): Someday your children...

or your children's children...

will hear stories about...

The Takeout Food Order.

One hundred thousand White Castle hamburgers...

recently sent two thousand miles...

from the midwest to White Castle lovers...

in Arizona,...

where they're not normally available.

Could just any hamburger...

inspire this kind of loyalty?

No. But then a White Castle...

is no ordinary hamburger.

Thank goodness they're available...

near us.

195T-a

Exhibit 4.5.

outside of the White Castle trading area, commercials end with this tag line: "Hamburgers to Fly. Call 1-800-W CASTLE."

Sale of Publications

Name a major news publication—*Time, Newsweek, U.S. News, the Wall Street Journal*—and a TV subscription commercial is almost certain to come to mind. The offers vary, the commercials vary in technique. But they are all the same in one regard: Each commercial encourages the viewer to subscribe by calling a toll-free number.

The ongoing success of news publications on TV is easily understood. Potential subscribers are consistent watchers of the nightly news. The news publications, each in their own way, give the viewer the opportunity to get the news behind the news. Calling an 800 number is a simple and easy way to fulfill that desire.

The Basics of Direct Response TV

It is not the mission of the authors to tell the reader how to create direct-response TV commercials, or when or where to run such commercials. Such matters are best left to direct-response advertising agencies who specialize in direct-response commercials.

However, we do believe it is in order to note some of the basics of direct-response commercials for which there seems to be general agreement among the experts.

1. Frequent mention and display of the telephone number is essential to success.
2. Dramatic demonstration of product benefits grabs and holds viewer interest.
3. Tests prove that most direct-response TV commercials are more cost-efficient when run during passive viewing periods such as when watching late-night movies. (Viewers are more prone to go to the phone during such periods.)
4. It is rarely possible to successfully complete the sale of a product in a commercial in less than a 90- to 120-second time period.

TELEMARKETING AND INTERACTIVE TV

Interactive TV is still in the developmental stage, but Telemarketing is interlaced with its future. Many systems are being tested, including QUBE, an interactive cable system developed by Warner Amex.

Viewtron, a joint venture of Knight-Ridder and AT&T, will serve to illustrate the potential of interactive TV and Telemarketing. The Viewtron system is vastly different than regular TV or cable in that there are no programs or shows as such. Instead, the viewer brings information on the screen on *command.*

Sports scores. Market reports. Local and national news. Any time of day or night ... on command. What's more, the subscriber can make bank transfers and pay bills with his or her Viewtron equipment.

Advertising potential is exciting. Say that you are a French food buff. You want to investigate French restaurants. You simply use your hand-held console and presto—here's a French restaurant, the menu, the prices, the address and phone number, plus credit card information (see Exhibit 4.6).

Or say that you are planning to fly to New York from Miami—you can check current competitive fares and order tickets from home. The same with hotels, rental cars, and so on. Telemarketing is an integral part of the system. Future potential boggles the mind.

TELEMARKETING AND RADIO

Regular TV and cable lend themselves to dramatic product demonstrations. Radio cannot. But there is a place for radio as a medium for promoting phone-in requests and phone-in orders.

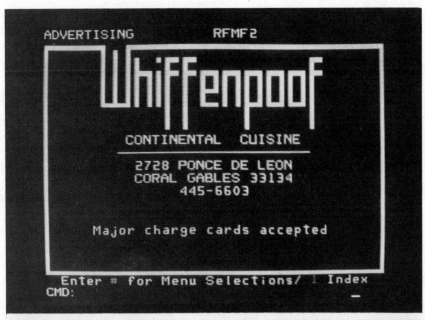

Exhibit 4.6.

Radio has two things going for it over regular TV: (1) program formats to which advertisers can better target; (2) much lower costs for like time periods.

Targeting to the right program formats is the key secret. For example, if an advertiser is soliciting phone-in orders for a rock album or tape, there's no problem running a radio commercial on scores of stations that feature rock music, the listeners being the very audience the advertiser is seeking.

Or if a financial advertiser is soliciting inquiries from potential investors, there are program formats that help him reach his target audience: Wall Street Report, for example, or FM stations with a high percentage of upper-income listeners.

This sixty-second radio commercial by Merrill Lynch was run in conjunction with program formats with a high percentage of listeners who match their customer profile.

(MUSIC UP AND UNDER)

ANNCR: A word on money management from Merrill Lynch. Today, many banks are trying to copy our revolutionary Cash Management Account financial service. Here's why they can't. Bank money market accounts are simply that: bank accounts. A Merrill Lynch CMA gives you access to the entire *range* of our investment opportunities. Instead of just an account, you get an Account Executive, backed by the top-ranked research team on Wall Street. Idle cash is automatically invested in your choice of *three* CMA money market funds. You enjoy check writing, a special VISA card, automatic variable rate loans up to the full margin loan value of your securities—at *rates* banks aren't likely to match. So give your money sound management, and *more* to grow on. The all-in-one CMA financial service. (MUSIC) From Merrill Lynch. A breed apart.

LOCAL ANNCR: For more complete information and a free prospectus, including sales charges and expenses, call 000-0000. Read it carefully before you invest or send money. That's 000-0000.

TELEMARKETING AND PRINT ADVERTISING

It is so common today to see in newspapers and magazines ads that feature either a local number or 800 number to get information or to place an order. (The 800 number service was first introduced in 1967.) And it is the 800 number that has changed the way many marketers do business. All to the good.

Examples of print advertising with the use of local and 800 numbers abound.

Let us zero in on just a few unusual applications.

Financial Advertising

It's not unusual for consumers to order merchandise by phone in the $10 to $100 range. But it is most unusual for consumers to order gold or silver by phone in units of $1,500, $2,500, $5,000, $10,000, and more. And yet they do in the aggregate of millions of dollars. By phone!

Exhibit 4.7 is typical of the sort of advertisement that Monex International runs consistently in the *Wall Street Journal* and other publications appealing to the serious investor. The ad has a distinctive oval shape, designed to make it stand out from competitive advertising

Exhibit 4.7.

along with direct-response copy.* Note that a great deal of importance is placed on the toll-free numbers (both the national and statewide 800 numbers are prominently featured) to expedite the response. A bonus offer is added to reinforce and reward an immediate phone response. Should the prospect wish to respond by mail through use of the coupon, both the home and the business phone numbers are requested to simplify the telephone *follow-up procedure.*

Another financial advertiser adept at Telemarketing techniques in print advertising is Merrill Lynch. Note how prominently they feature their local telephone numbers in newspaper advertising in the state of California. They too ask for the business and home phone numbers should the prospect wish to mail the coupon. (Exhibit 4.8).

Not to be outdone by brokerage firms and dealers in precious metal, banks are also getting on the Telemarketing bandwagon.

John F. Cooley, president of Merchandise National Bank of Chicago, is a strong advocate of soliciting phone inquiries in his print advertising. His most unique service is a 24-hour Rate Line. Copy featuring the Rate Line reads as follows:

Get on the "Rate Line"
  Call 836-8085
For Daily Quotes on:
    —IRA Money Rate Certificates
    —6-month Money Market
      Certificates of Deposit
    —$100,000 Minimum Time Deposit
      Rates for 30, 60 and 90 days.

Merchandise National Bank of Chicago
Merchandise Mart
Apparel Center
Germania Club Building

Callers to the Rate Line get a recorded message giving the rates for that particular day. Categories covered include money market funds, super NOW accounts, six-month C.D.s, ninety-one-day C.D.s, $100,000 C.D.s, and IRA certificates.

Many major banks have assigned officers to Telemarketing functions such as account solicitation and cross-selling activities. Activities such as selling $100,000 C.D.s to major depositors, financing of automobile fleets to commercial accounts, etc. The more account information banks punch into their databases, the easier telephone cross-selling becomes. By assigning bank officers to blocks of accounts a customer rapport is soon established.

*With AT&T 800 Single Number Service it is no longer necessary to have two separate 800 numbers, one for interstate and one for intrastate. One number can now be used for both.

NOW THE BIGGEST SELECTION OF CDs YOU CAN FIND IS JUST AROUND THE CORNER.

Here, in Southern California, Merrill Lynch is *the* place to shop for CDs or CD Participations. Our programs include as complete a range as you can find anywhere, with maturities from six months to 14 years.

CD Participations. Merrill Lynch pioneered these participations in jumbo CDs. Fixed-rate CDPs pay higher than bank money market certificates; variable-rate CDPs float above Donoghue's Money Fund Average.™

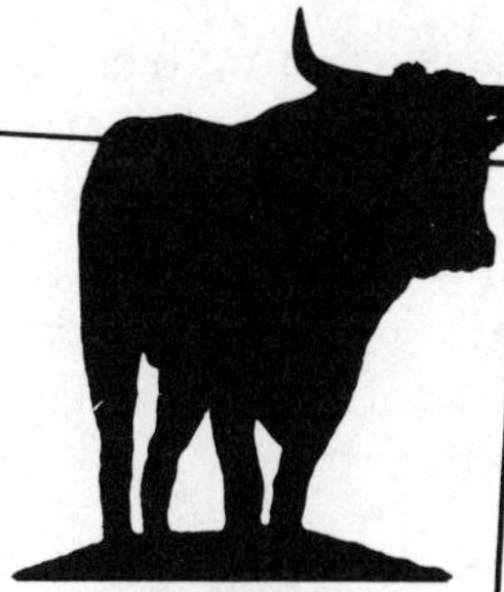

Medium and long-term CDs. Locked-in interest rates, the safety of FDIC or FSLIC insurance, and semiannual interest payments make these CDs ideal for savings. Maturities range from 2½ to 10 years.

Zero Coupon CDs. Ideal investments for IRA, Keogh and other tax-advantaged accounts.

At maturity you receive a lump-sum payment of two, three or four times your investment.

These CDs and CD Participations are covered by more FDIC or SLIC insurance than available at any bank.

Because when you buy through Merrill Lynch, you get the added advantage of access to the largest secondary market for CDs in the industry.

If you need your money prior to maturity, you can sell at the prevailing market price, and avoid the substantial interest penalty typically associated with early redemption at a bank.

While not obligated to do so, Merrill Lynch has maintained and fully intends to continue maintaining this secondary market.

No one else can give you more help with more kinds of investments. No one else.

29 WAYS TO TALK TO NUMBER ONE*

Beverly Hills 213 858-4600
Century City 213 858-4700
East Long Beach 213 594-4771
Escondido 619 741-1212
Fullerton 714 879-4322
Glendale 213 240-7600
Hollywood 213 468-8100
Laguna Hills 714 859-2900
La Jolla 619 459-2311
La Mesa 619 697-4219
Long Beach 213 435-3771
L.A./Wilshire 213 488-2334
L.A./6th Street 213 488-2611
Newport Beach 714 955-6000
Orange/Anaheim 714 978-2770
Palm Springs 619 325-8611
Pasadena 213 356-2000
Riverside 714 686-2442
San Bernardino 714 884-9246
San Diego 619 235-7500
San Marino 213 285-0491
Santa Ana 714 547-7272
Santa Barbara 805 963-0333
Santa Monica 213 451-2591
Sherman Oaks 213 995-5600
Torrance 213 540-6222
Thousand Oaks 805 497-0390 or 213 889-2600
Ventura/Oxnard 805 659-1900
Westwood 213 470-7000

Mail to: Merrill Lynch Operations Center
P.O. Box 6054, Inglewood, CA 90312

Please send me your free booklet on Insured CDs.

Name ______

Address ______

City ______ State ______ Zip ______

Business Phone ______ Home Phone ______

Merrill Lynch customers, please give name and office address of Account Executive:

______

Merrill Lynch
Merrill Lynch Pierce Fenner & Smith Inc.
A breed apart.

Exhibit 4.8.

Dealer Locater Advertising

Examples of Telemarketing techniques applied to print advertising continue.

Consider the problem a major marketer with hundreds or thousands of dealers faces when a very special service is offered only through a select number of their dealers. Telemarketing turns out to be the ideal solution.

The Chevron ad in Exhibit 4.9 is a classic example of the solution. Note how Chevron makes it easy for the consumer to learn the name and address of the nearest dealer offering "6-Point Car Service Warranty Protection."

More and more national advertisers are offering a dealer locater service by providing a toll-free number in their print advertising. It's faster, more economical, and more cost-efficient.

TELEMARKETING AND MULTIMEDIA

While examples thus far relate to applications of Telemarketing to specific mediums, it should be noted that applications lend themselves equally to total campaigns, using more than one medium. Blue Cross and Blue Shield of Southwestern Virginia is a classic example of an organization who applied Telemarketing in a multimedia campaign.

Effective July 1, 1983, the Virginia General Assembly eliminated the boundaries of the territories of the two Blue Cross and Blue Shield Plans operating in the state. This meant the plans could now compete with each other.

Blue Cross and Blue Shield of Southwestern Virginia in Roanoke was David; Blue Cross and Blue Shield of Virginia in Richmond was the giant Goliath. The Richmond Plan was established in sixty-eight more populous counties, was five times larger in number of policyholders, had a considerably larger financial base and the preeminent name in the state.

The opportunity to compete was exciting, but the odds against scoring over firmly entrenched competition—not only the Richmond Plan, but other health-care group plans as well—were staggering, to say the least.

Houch & Harrison Advertising, Marketing and Public Relations of Roanoke, Virginia was charged with developing a campaign that would establish the Roanoke Plan throughout the state. The agency developed a creative strategy that utilized Telemarketing to create immediate awareness. The number "1-800-542-BLUE" became both the vehicle and

CHEVRON DEALERS SAY... Yes

6-Point Car Service Warranty Protection

While many gas stations are saying no to choices and services, Chevron Dealers say Yes. Yes to a *6-point warranty protection plan* on many car care services at Chevron Hallmark Award Stations.

1. **90 DAYS or 4,000 MILES GUARANTEED**
Whichever comes first. Warranty covers all parts and labor.

2. **PROBLEM SOLVED OR MONEY REFUNDED**
If a problem occurs, either the work will be done over at no cost to you, or the entire cost will be refunded, at the dealer's option.

3. **ADVANCE WRITTEN ESTIMATES**
You'll know the cost before work begins. If additional repairs are needed, your approval will be obtained first.

4. **RETURN OF REPLACED PARTS**
At your request, all replaced parts will be returned for your inspection.

5. **HONORED AT HALLMARK AWARD STATIONS WITH REPAIR FACILITIES**
If a problem occurs, take your car back to the station where the service was performed. If you're more than 50 miles from that station, your warranty will be honored by any Hallmark Award Dealer who performs that type of service.

6. **ON-THE-ROAD HOTLINE**
There are over 1000 Hallmark Award Dealers with service facilities in the U.S. You can call toll-free **(800) 227-1677** for the nearest station which will honor your warranty.

You'll find that all Chevron Hallmark Award Dealers— including those who do not offer car care service— maintain the highest standards of customer service.
For the nearest Chevron Hallmark Award Station call:

(800) 227-1677

Complete Details of Warranty available at your Chevron Hallmark Award Station.

Exhibit 4.9.

identity for individuals to contact Blue Cross and Blue Shield of Southwestern Virginia from anywhere in the state.

The media mix consisted of all television for two weeks, followed by radio for a week, followed by outdoor advertising and newspaper and magazine advertising. (Exhibit 4.10 shows the magazine ad.) Only the toll-free number appeared on TV, radio, and in outdoor advertising: the coupon with address was used only in print media.

Results from the campaign were extraordinary. The "Out of the Blue" campaign helped the Roanoke Plan to realize a 12.5% net growth rate in subscribers in 1983, making it the fastest growing Blue Cross and Blue Shield Plan in the nation.

TELEMARKETING AND CATALOGS

Of all the advertising applications of the 800 number none have proved more successful than toll-free phone order privileges for catalog buyers. Catalog director after catalog director reports the average phone order to be 20% greater than the average mail order. Thus, if a catalog firm gets an average order of $70 by mail, they can expect an average phone order of $84.

The reason for the larger order is easy to explain. A woman ordering a dress by phone, for example, puts the telephone communicator into a natural consultative selling situation. Consider this dialogue:

> Fine, Mrs. Smith. You want size 18 in the royal blue. Have you considered the scarf on page 32, item #1628? This would really look beautiful with the royal blue. —Good. I'll include it with your order. Shipment will go out via UPS tonight. Thank you.

Some catalog firms have developed consultative selling to a high degree. Talbots' of Hingham, Maine, for example, has developed an innovative way to make all their telephone communicators familiar with the apparel they sell. They have installed a moving dress rack adjacent to their telephone center. So when a customer calls and asks a question, the telephone communicator only needs to press a button. Presto—the apparel in question is in her hands. And she can answer questions in an authoritative and meaningful way.

Consultative selling increases the average catalog order. No doubt about it. But here is another unique way to increase the average phone order: Jack Schmid, a catalog consultant in Kansas City, Missouri, came

NOW, FROM OUT OF THE BLUE, INNOVATIVE GROUP BENEFITS FOR ALL OF VIRGINIA.

1-800-542-BLUE

Call toll free anywhere in Virginia to discover what's new in Blue Cross and Blue Shield benefits.

When it comes to giving companies of 2 or more people better health care programs, we aim high. That's why, out of the blue, we're offering innovative programs all over Virginia. And, in areas of the state where we've never been before.

With our Comprehensive Health Care Plans, you get flexibility in financing and benefits. So your coverage is customized to give you only the services you desire. At a low deductible. And low price.

Even if your needs are presently covered, you'll want to know how we can brighten the outlook of your future health care plans.

Send the coupon for a free brochure. Or, call and investigate the competitive differences we offer.

You'll find the best plans come right out of the blue: Toll free 1-800-542-BLUE.

Yes, I want to know how innovative a Comprehensive Health Care Plan can be today. Please send me your free brochure. No obligation.

Name

Company Name

Address

City _____ State _____ Zip _____

Number of employees _____ Phone _____

For Virginia groups only.

Mail to: Blue Cross and Blue Shield of Southwestern Virginia
P. O. Box 13047, Roanoke, Virginia 24045

Blue Cross Blue Shield
of Southwestern Virginia
Roanoke

® Registered Marks Blue Cross and Blue Shield Association

83-425-5-AA

Exhibit 4.10.

up with this idea when he was catalog manager of Halls, a division of Hallmark.

Jack printed the following legend in his catalog - "When you place your order by phone, ask our telephone communicator for the special of the week." Dialogue between the customer and the telephone communicator went along these lines.

CUSTOMER: I'd like to order items #1202 and #1842. Also, I'd like to know what your special of the week is.

COMMUNICATOR: Our special of the week is the set of six tumblers on page 21. If you will turn to that page you will note that the catalog price is $24. Our special price this week is $18.

CUSTOMER: Okay. Add the tumblers to my order.

This program was a great success. Depending upon the special of the week, up to 29% of those who placed phone orders added the special of the week to their orders.

Promoting Phone Orders

Because catalog phone orders are so desirable, it behooves the catalog marketer to promote the service in an effective way. Multiple use of a telephone symbol in the catalog along with toll-free numbers is the preferred way. And the toll-free number should always be featured on the order form, large enough to attract proper attention, of course (Exhibit 4.11).

There are no standards for the number of times the 800 number should be featured. But a good rule-of-thumb is once every four pages.

Particular note should be made of the appeal "24 hours a day, 7 days a week." This is customer service to the nth degree. And when we consider today's life styles, logic says the maximum service is worth the investment.

With dual-income families on the rise, catalog shopping occurs primarily during evening hours and over weekends. Many catalog purchases are impulse purchases. So the opportunity to pick up the phone any hour, any day, to place an order has great appeal. And there's just something about placing an order at midnight that seems bizarre and satisfying!

THE GALLERY

O F   A M S T E R D A M

G-9-83

CREDIT CARD HOLDERS!
CALL TOLL FREE: DEPT. #6799
24 hrs. a day, 7 days a week 1 800 833-2008
New York Residents Call 1 800 342-6116
Please have your Catalog and Credit Card readily available.

Please print. Most orders will arrive prepaid via United Parcel, sometimes in more than one shipment. We also will notify you of unusual delays. Please allow additional time for monogramming.

□ Mr.   □ Mrs.   □ Miss   □ Ms.   please print

Your Name _____

Address _____

City _____

State _____ Zip _____

Telephone and Area Code (_____) _____

If A Gift Please Tell Us Where To Ship _____

□ Mr.   □ Mrs.   □ Miss   □ Ms.   please print

Name _____

Address _____

City _____

State _____ Zip _____

QTY	CATALOG NUMBER	ITEM NAME	SIZE	COLOR CHOICE 1st	2nd	CATALOG PRICE EACH	TOTAL

Monogram (Initials)
As you wish it to appear.

Merchandise Total

Add Postage, Handling & Insurance

Total Order	$15.00 & under	$15.01 to $30.	$30.01 to $50.	$50.01 & over
Postage, Handling & Insurance	$2.35	$3.95	$5.25	$6.75

ENCLOSE CHECK OR MONEY ORDER FOR TOTAL AMOUNT
or charge to one of the listed accounts.
□ Master Card   □ Visa   □ American Express   □ Check   □ Money Order

Account No. _____ Bank # _____
(Note: $15 minimum order on All Credit Card Charges.) List all numbers shown above or below your name on Credit Card.

Account Address (if different than address above) _____

Account Expiration Date (if shown on card) _____

Signature _____

Telephone and Area Code (_____) _____

N.Y. State Residents
Add appropriate tax

ADD $1.00 FOR EACH
ADDITIONAL MAILING ADDRESS

TOTAL

Thank you for your order

Exhibit 4.11.

SPECIFIC 800 DISPLAY GUIDELINES

Whether you display your 800 number in print or on TV—in advertising, promotion, or on stationery—do it the right way. Here are six useful guidelines to follow:

1. The 800 CODE. Remember: Always show 800 as an integral, inseparable part of your 800 service number. Use bold print for all 800 numbers and always include "1" before 800.

    1 800 555-2638

2. INSTATE 800 ALTERNATIVE NUMBER. AT&T 800 Single Number Service allows callers instate and out of your home state to call the same number. If you do not have this service, include an alternate instate 800 number for home state callers. Since the numbers are different, show both 800 numbers. For local callers, include your regular number.

Call us toll-free:	1 800 555-2638
In New York State call toll-free:	1 800 555-1234
For local calls in New York City:	555-5678

3. OTHER ALTERNATE NUMBERS. If you don't have a statewide 800 Service number, you can still encourage in-state customers by offering to accept collect calls. Include the Area Code if your state has more than one Area Code. It's a good idea to repeat your regular number without area code for local callers.

Call us toll free:	1 800 555-1100
In Illinois call collect:	0 312 555-4567
For local calls in Chicago:	555-4567

4. HOURS AVAILABLE: Specify the hours during which operators are on duty to answer calls at your 800 number. Include the time zone. If the number is answered 24 hours a day, then there is an advantage to stating this.

Call toll free	
Between 8 A.M. and 6 P.M. (P.S.T.)	1 800 555-6520
Call toll free	
Available 24 hours a day	1 800 555-6520

5. AVAILABLE AREAS. It may not be feasible or efficient to provide an 800 Service number for all geographic areas reached by your advertising. In such a case, indicate where callers can dial your 800 number.

Call toll-free:	
In Colorado, Iowa, Missouri, Nebraska	
and Oklahoma, call:	1 800 555-2368
In Kansas, call:	1 800 555-6677
Elsewhere, call collect:	0 316 555-7890

6. EXCLUDED AREAS. If you do not have distribution—or if your product or service is not available—in certain areas which may be in your advertising "reach," note this to avoid needless calls that can tie up your 800 number.

Call us toll-free:	1 800 555-0000
In Connecticut, call toll-free:	1 800 555-6666
In Hartford, call:	555-2368
Not available in New York State	

In addition, if your advertising is seen outside the continental United States, be sure to specify points from which your 800 number cannot be used. AT&T 800 Service is available from some offshore points.

TELEMARKETING AND DIRECT MAIL

Telemarketers learned early on that if you give direct-mail recipients the choice of either making a toll-free call or returning a reply card total response is usually increased. And AT&T has found, as have many others, that those who inquire by phone are more likely to order. Exhibit 4.12 is a good example of how AT&T long-distance services emphasize their toll-free number in both their letter and reply card. Note too that the respondent is asked to provide a phone number when responding, thus speeding up the response time on the part of AT&T.

While thousands of firms have now adopted the practice of offering toll-free call privileges to prospects, far fewer have established a toll-free "Hot Line" number to existing customers, the life blood of their business. The opportunity to enhance goodwill is great, for a toll-free "Hot Line" number gives the customer special recognition and strengthens the buyer-seller relationship.

We spoke earlier about the Rate Line, conceived by John Cooley, president of the Merchandise National Bank of Chicago. He features the Rate Line number in his print advertising, but he doesn't stop there. Exhibit 4.13 shows the front panel of a statement insert. What better source for promoting a bank service?

In Chapter 6, we will go into lead generation programs in depth. But it's not too early to point out the advantages of intermixing phone and mail response options in relation to lead generation.

There are two points that should be established at this time: (1) If you offer the prospect the option of returning a business reply card or

AT&T

2301 Main Street • P.O. Box 549 • Kansas City, Missouri 64141 • 1 800 821-2121, ext. 626

Dear Executive,

We are pleased to be able to present our special AT&T long distance services in one comprehensive "Business Services Guide."

This gives you the opportunity to review just what the new AT&T is offering. From AT&T Long Distance Service to AT&T Data Services, we bring you the best telecommunications network anywhere.

Our services are designed to help your business grow, and grow with your business, no matter how small or large your company is.

And along with the thorough outline of our services in your enclosed Business Services Guide, we're also offering a free consultation with a professional Consultant, to help you choose the AT&T long distance services that are right for you.

Simply call us toll-free at 1 800 821-2121, ext. 626 to speak to an AT&T Network Consultant.

Our Consultants have worked with businesses of all sizes across the country, so we can help you decide which services make sense for your company. And your Consultant will offer personalized service and advice to help your business use them to cut costs, increase your sales, and help your business grow faster. He or she can even coordinate implementation of the services for you.

So take some time to read through your Business Services Guide. And be sure to contact your Network Consultant at our toll-free number, or mail the enclosed postpaid card, to put these services to work for your business.

Sincerely,

Judy DeVooght

Judy DeVooght
Manager, Network Consultants

FIND OUT HOW YOUR BUSINESS CAN CUT COSTS AND IMPROVE PROFITABILITY WITH AT&T LONG DISTANCE SERVICES

CALL TOLL-FREE

1 800 821-2121, ext. 626
OR MAIL THIS POSTPAID CARD

YES! Please tell me more about AT&T long distance services.

Please fill in Phone Number _____
(Area Code)

If address is incorrect, fill out information below.

Name/Title _____
Company _____
Address _____
City _____ State _____ Zip _____

33U-073

Exhibit 4.12. Illustration of a letter from AT&T with a reply card.

Get a
tax-free
retirement
gift

from your
rich Uncle.

**You, too, will appreciate the
new up-to-$4,000 a year
tax deduction — and you'll
really like our extra
IRA interest!**

CALL OUR 24-HOUR RATE LINE

836-8085

FOR THE LATEST MONEY RATE CERTIFICATE QUOTATIONS

Exhibit 4.13.

inquiry via an 800 number, total response from the mailing is likely to be as much as 20% greater than if the only option is to return a business reply card; and (2) Closures (sales) from those who inquire by phone are likely to be as much as two times greater than those who inquire by mail. These estimates are based upon research conducted by AT&T, covering over 20 million lead generation mailing pieces.

TELEMARKETING AND PACKAGE GOODS

Telemarketing and Yellow Pages advertising. Telemarketing and TV, radio, print, catalogs, and direct mail. We've covered all the media except one—package goods.

The package is a medium. A dynamic medium. Typically, every package gives two pieces of information: (1) ingredients, and (2) directions for use. But what happens if the customer wonders if the product can be used for something not indicated, or doesn't understand the directions?

One need look no further than to Procter & Gamble—master marketer—to see the value of carrying an 800 number on package goods. P&G began testing 800 numbers on their packages in 1974. By 1979, it was decided to print 800 numbers on all P&G consumer products, and this goal was accomplished by 1981.

In a recent twelve-month period, P&G had over 200,000 customer contacts. About two-thirds of these were by phone. Typical of answers to consumer queries are these.

"Crisco may be used for six to nine months after it is opened. It has an indefinite shelf-life if the product is unopened."

"Your food may not be browning because the pan is overcrowded or because the temperature is too low. 365° is recommended for frying: 375° for deep frying."

"Downy can cause stains if it is spilled directly onto a fabric. But, the stains can generally be removed by dampening the area, rubbing the stain with a bar of soap and rinsing."

"Downy has no more effect on flame retardant properties than does washing with a regular detergent."

"Prell is helpful in removing loose dandruff flakes from the hair. It's not designed, though, to control severe or persistent dandruff. Such problems require special anti-dandruff products like Head and Shoulders."

"Many people with color treated hair use Prell with complete satisfaction. The removal of color from color treated hair is generally not significantly affected by the brand of shampoo used."

Market research on the addition of an 800 number of P&G package goods indicates that 90% of consumers are satisfied with phone response. Of equal importance, they indicate they will continue to use the product they called about.

The 800 number has closed the gap between the consumer and the package goods company. Bigness and remoteness have melted down to one-on-one communication.

But one-on-one communication is not limited to package goods companies. The same potential exists for hard goods companies. Let's listen in on a taped message Steve Upton, V.P. Consumer Affairs, The Whirlpool Corporation, gave AT&T about their Cool Line service.

"Hello. Thank you for calling. I'm Steve Upton, Vice President of Consumer Affairs for the Whirlpool Corporation. It was in 1967 that we really pushed to get our Cool Line service installed. And are we glad we did!

"What's the Cool Line? That's our name for Whirlpool's 800 number. We use the 800 service nationwide as a way of promoting and maintaining a line of communication with customers using our products. Now the purpose? To answer the consumers' questions and help them solve product service problems.

"Now, we've really done this up right. We've placed some of our most experienced technical personnel at the receiving end of the 800 numbers. This way, many performance problems are solved right on the phone. In fact, 93% of the calls are taken care of over the telephone. The remaining 7% result in referrals to one of our consumer affairs district offices.

"Do you know what that means in terms of service calls that are avoided? In 1983, we estimate we saved our customers almost three-quarters of a million dollars and we saved *ourselves* over $500,000 on unnecessary calls to customers who are still in-warranty. That savings more than pays for the 800 line.

"But there are *more* benefits:

1. A good first experience by the customer results in additional product sales.
2. With the Cool Line weeding out unnecessary service calls, response time for service calls is cut. And because preliminary

problem identification is obtained by the Cool Line, service technicians are better equipped to solve the problem on the first visit.

3. Most importantly—consumer activist groups, which have hurt many corporate images, have praised Whirlpool for its Cool Line consumer program. Yes—in an age of consumerism backlash, Whirlpool has enjoyed growing corporate respect in the marketplace!

"We put our 800 number on every Whirlpool appliance, warranty, use and care guide, and in all of our sales literature. We *want* our customers to call if they have questions or problems. It certainly makes them feel better about dealing with us!

"If you or your customer could benefit by bringing the company closer to the consumer in this way, consider an 800 number.

"800 is a very important number at Whirlpool."

Telemarketing is now as much a part of the advertising process as is market planning. Telemarketing can provide the edge every advertiser needs.

CHAPTER 5

Telemarketing in the Sales Promotion Process

Sales Promotion: Sales promotion is an incentive to buy which the seller offers the potential buyer other than the product itself ... with the objective of creating immediate sales, or accelerating the decision-making process.

The above is the official definition of sales promotion as defined by Richard Hagle, publisher of the widely read sales promotion newsletter *Sales Promotion Monitor.*

Examples of time-honored promotion techniques include sweepstakes, cents-off coupons, product demonstrations, and product use information. But now a new technique has been added to the sales promotion arsenal: sales promotion involving 800 and 900 number phone calls.

Involvement is key to all sales promotion techniques: entering a sweepstakes to see if you have won; redeeming cents-off coupons to save; participating in product demonstrations; learning the uses you can apply for a given product or service. The involvement uniquely inherent in a phone call adds a dimension with exciting potential.

Because the phone call involvement technique is so new, we believe the best way to explore the possibilities is by live examples of applications. Not only do these examples illustrate techniques, but they show how promotions might be targeted against specific objectives as well.

PROMOTIONS USING AN 800 NUMBER

Increasing Market Share

Our first case history is about one of the most sensational sales promotion campaigns of past decades—The Quaker Oats CAP'N CRUNCH "Find La Foote" sweepstakes.

The Market Situation

There are over 100 different brands of cereal in the marketplace. At the time of the promotion, CAP'N CRUNCH was an eighteen-year-old brand in the mature stage of its product life cycle.

Objective

The objective of the campaign was twofold: (1) Generate trial and child interest in the brand, and (2) increase market share.

The Campaign

Quaker Oats developed a promotion in which specially marked boxes of CAP'N CRUNCH contained a hideout map indicating various locations where the pirate LaFoote had buried his treasure. This was an inpack premium, meaning simply that the hideout map was inside the box of cereal. Promotional support for the campaign included 25-cents-off coupons, television ads, floor displays, shelf talkers, and a special television commercial that communicated the promotion to children. (See Figure 5.1.)

Involvement

One of the keys to any successful sales promotion is to generate involvement of the target audience. It was at this juncture that the CAP'N CRUNCH promotion took a twist—a creative twist that pushed responses and sales to a much greater level than expected.

To add excitement and immediate involvement with the children, Quaker Oats provided an 800 number for them to call to find out LaFoote's correct location. If the location mentioned on the taped

Exhibit 5.1. Newspaper insert used in the CAP'N CRUNCH campaign.

message matched the location indicated on the map inside of their cereal box, the child won a Huffy bicycle.

Now just imagine the anticipation of an emotionally charged youngster dialing the 800 number to find out instantly whether or not he or she is a winner! Incredible!

Results

The results of this promotion were just that—incredible. Over 24 million calls were registered in a four-month period. In fact, the original number of 800 lines were insufficient to handle the volume. More lines were needed.

The end result of this promotion was that CAP'N CRUNCH exploded in market share from 2.9 to 3.9, a very significant increase in a very large category. The 33% increase in market share during the promotion was unprecedented in the industry. Most importantly, even after the promotion CAP'N CRUNCH maintained an increased market share.

Obviously, the CAP'N CRUNCH promotion was a big success. As a matter of fact, *Advertising Age*, the country's leading advertising journal, voted the Quaker Oats promotion to be one of the best sales promotions of the year.

Gaining Shelf and Floor Space

There is a never-ending battle in the retail arena. The eternal battle is to gain more shelf and floor space, particularly more floor space. Competition is fierce. Getting favorable space is very much dependent upon increasing consumer demand.

Johnnie Walker Red, a leading brand of scotch, increased consumer demand substantially by devising a simple contest involving the telephone. (Total prizes equalled $50,000.) The consumer was given the opportunity to win $25,000 by simply picking up the telephone, dialing an 800 toll-free number, and listening to a question. The answer to that question could be found on any bottle of Johnnie Walker Red.

The taped message was delivered with a Scottish brogue. Here is what the consumer heard:

> JOHNNIE (Scottish Brogue): Hello, you've reached the Johnnie Walker Red "Hot Line"! I'm glad you called to find out the question in our $50,000 Johnnie Walker Red "Hot Line" Contest. Here it is: Name the city in Scotland where Johnnie Walker Red is bottled. And to show you what a good sport I am, I'll even give you a clue where to find the answer—turn to Red in your liquor store or call for Red at your favorite bar, because the answer's on the label of any bottle of Johnnie Walker Red, the scotch that's the world's favorite. Now, here's the question again: Name the city in Scotland where Johnnie Walker Red is bottled. My thanks for calling—and best of luck!

Since this campaign is history, we are free to give you the answer to the question "In what city in Scotland is Johnnie Walker Red bottled?" The answer is Kilmarnock.

Results

Johnnie Walker Red generated almost one million entries in the contest. Sales increased about 20%, thus earning more favorable floor space. This campaign was so successful, as a matter of fact, that Johnnie Walker ran similar campaigns for two subsequent years following the original campaign.

The Johnnie Walker campaign involved the consumer in an effort to gain precious floor space. But Gordon's Gin took another route to accomplish the same objective; Gordon's went directly to the retail liquor store owner with their promotion, emphasizing profit potential. Specifically, Gordon's wanted to gain endcap displays on the aisle—the choicest of display space.

This sales promotion campaign was called "The African Scene" and it was patterned after the movie "The African Queen" with Humphrey Bogart. Gordon's used some outtakes of the film, showing Bogie opening up a case of Gordon's Gin and taking out a bottle. The objective of the promotion was to get the retail liquor dealer to order the display (see Exhibit 5.2) and to surround it with cases of Gordon's Gin.

To bring off the theme of the promotion, Gordon's hired a Humphrey Bogart impersonator—Robert Sachi—to tape a message that the retail liquor store owner heard when he called the toll-free 800 number. Here is the profitability message that was heard:

How ya doing, sweetheart? This is your old pal from the African Scene. You guys and gals in the liquor trade, you've got it made this

Exhibit 5.2. Gordon's Gin display.

summer. You've got my kisser on the new Gordon's Gin poster display. Your customers will snap up these free posters fast, just as they will Gordon's Gin. This display has a pad of 25 posters of me and Gordon's. I don't have to tell you, floor displays generate four to seven times more sales than shelf displays. I'll be pulling for you, but it's up to you, baby, to do your part too. Put plenty of Gordon's around the display and watch the sales grow and sure as the summer is long, me and Gordon's are number one with your customers. Well, here's looking at you, sweetheart, and the hottest summer sale success you ever had.

Results

Gordon's received 3,000 responses from the trade. They placed 13,000 displays against a normal placement of 5,000 to 6,000. Sales increased by 26% in a sales period during which gin sales to the retail liquor store would normally be in a downward trend.

Lead Generation

Lead generation, producing qualified leads, is integral to Telemarketing. (See Chapter 6, Telemarketing in the Selling Process.) Lee Hill of Chicago, Illinois came up with an unique way to get leads from business people for their high-ticket program by devising an "Executive Scratch Game."

Lee Hill's target market was 1,500 selected senior marketing executives. Each received a very creative direct mail piece (see Exhibit 5.3). The executive was invited to scratch off three—and only three—of the Touchtone numbers involved in the game.

If the symbols matched, the executive was invited to scratch off the prize box. Having scratched off the prize box, the mail recipient was then invited to call 1-800-LEE-HILL to determine whether or not he or she was an instant winner.

Let's listen to Lee Hill's message. And then we'll review the results.

Hi! This is Lee Hill and I want to thank you for taking part in our Telepromotion game. Telepromotion is a new technique that combines the advanced technology of the Bell Systems 800 and 900 numbers with an exciting and involving creative hook. It increases response and it increases sales, because it is personally involving. For instance, you got involved enough to find out if you're a winner and if you have three star symbols on your game sheet. Those three star symbols have won you a great ballpoint pen from Tiffany's. Just complete the prize claim form and mail it to us. If you have three

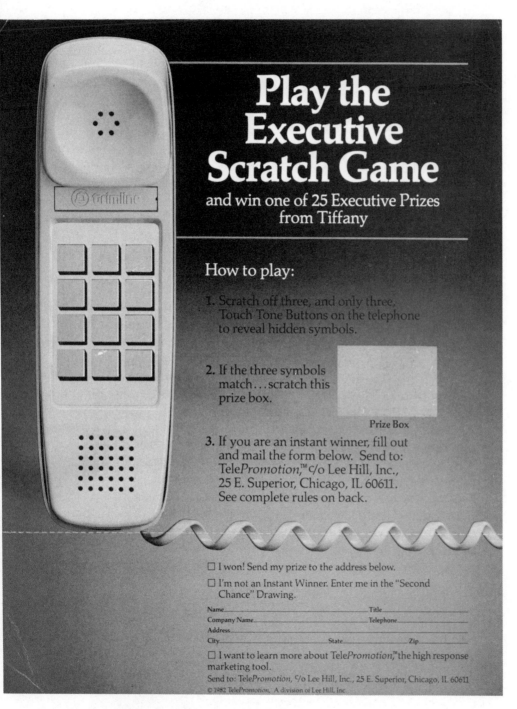

Play the Executive Scratch Game

and win one of 25 Executive Prizes from Tiffany

How to play:

1. Scratch off three, and only three, Touch Tone Buttons on the telephone to reveal hidden symbols.

2. If the three symbols match...scratch this prize box.

Prize Box

3. If you are an instant winner, fill out and mail the form below. Send to: TelePromotion,™ c/o Lee Hill, Inc., 25 E. Superior, Chicago, IL 60611. See complete rules on back.

☐ I won! Send my prize to the address below.

☐ I'm not an Instant Winner. Enter me in the "Second Chance" Drawing.

Name_____ Title_____
Company Name_____ Telephone_____
Address_____
City_____ State_____ Zip_____

☐ I want to learn more about TelePromotion,™ the high response marketing tool.

Send to: TelePromotion, c/o Lee Hill, Inc., 25 E. Superior, Chicago, IL 60611

© 1982 TelePromotion, A division of Lee Hill, Inc.

Exhibit 5.3. Illustration of Lee Hill direct-mail piece.

diamond symbols, you are not an instant winner, but you can still win a Tiffany pen in our second chance drawing. Send in your claim form and don't forget to check the Telepromotion box for information that can make you a big winner in promotion. All prize claim forms must be received by January 7, 1983. Mail now. We want you to be a winner.*

*Telepromotion (R). Registered trademark of Lee Hill, Inc. 1983

Results

Lee Hill received over 300 responses via the 800 number for a 20% response. In addition, there were over 120 second-chance entries requesting information for an additional 8% response. Total response was remarkable when compared to a normal direct-mail response which one could expect to be in the 2% to 5% range.

Brand Awareness

To the marketing director of a mass merchandiser, brand awareness figures are as important as Dow Jones averages are to the Wall Street analyst. Both want to see their figures go up.

In one of the most unique applications of Telemarketing to date, Dr Pepper Company used the phone for a dual purpose: (1) to increase entries into their $1 million sweepstakes promotion, and (2) to enhance awareness and trial of the brand.

The tactic Dr Pepper used was to call 150,000 potential consumers randomly. The calls were made during the six-week period of the sweepstakes promotion. Two trivia questions were asked of each: (1) Is there a period after "Dr" in "Dr Pepper"?, and (2) Is there a hyphen between "Sugar" and "Free" in "Sugar Free Dr Pepper"?

If respondents were able to answer either of the two questions correctly, they were automatically entered in the million-dollar sweepstakes. Regardless of answers, Dr Pepper sent a coupon for the product to each, thus enhancing brand awareness and product trial.

Results

Results were remarkable. Some 80% of those reached by phone had one or the other question correct. In all, they got 117,000 entries from the 150,000 households reached. (The answer to both trivia questions, by the way, is "no.")

Self-Liquidating Premiums

Self-liquidating premiums have always been a tried-and-true promotional device for the sales promotion specialist. They include mugs, pennants, lighters, pens, T-shirts, wallets, globes, calculators, film developing, radios—just to mention a few. And more recently—telephones.

Both the marketer and the consumer benefit from self-liquidating premiums. The marketer promotes the premium to hype the sales of his brand, but is reimbursed by the consumer for the cost of the premium: The consumer purchases the premium at a cost most often far below retail.

Coors beer, for example, fully appreciates the promotion value of self-liquidating premiums. One of their popular premiums was the Gordon Snidow posters depicting western scenes.

Orders for posters were always placed by mail. But Coors had a problem:

Consumers were looking for greater convenience in ordering than afforded by mail-in order forms. Coors decided to try to solve this problem by promoting an 800 number for ordering. Their secondary objective was to improve delivery times of the posters.

Results

The 800 number met both objectives. Phone-in orders represented over 25% of total orders, and these were probably incremental. Delivery time improved substantially.

Of course, not all premiums are self-liquidating. Parker Pen, for example, offered a $10 AT&T Gift Certificate for long-distance calling with the purchase of a pen and pencil set. Many other major marketers have offered AT&T Gift Certificates in varying amounts with proof of purchase.

New Brand Introductions

Mail sampling of package goods such as toothpaste, cereals, and detergents has been a ploy of marketers for decades. In recent years increased postage costs have put a damper on this sampling strategy. Cigarette companies, for example, went to distributing free samples on street corners and in shopping malls.

When Lorillard Inc., New York, wanted to get women nationwide to try its new Satin brand of cigarettes, they went beyond sample hand-outs. Lorillard ran a two-page, four-color print advertisement offering two free packs of Satin and a satin pouch to consumers who called an 800 toll-free number (see Exhibit 5.4).

When interviewed by *Direct Marketing Journal*, Sara Ridgway, vice-president/public relations at Lorillard Inc., commented, "In our wildest dreams we never anticipated what would happen. We ran out of the satin pouches we were offering."

Ridgway told the *Journal* that the tobacco firm who introduced Satin nationally in February 1983 tested the use of the 800 toll-free number offer in Denver and Milwaukee before rolling out nationally. Ridgway would not disclose the number of requests received, citing "competitive reasons." However, she did state that Lorillard enlisted hundreds of phone assistants to answer calls twenty-four hours a day.

The fact that consumers requested samples as contrasted to receiving samples without request makes a case for a higher percentage converting to this new brand. As Mrs. Ridgway concluded, "If you can get the product in the hands of consumers, it's the best shot you have of converting a smoker from one brand to another."

PROMOTIONS USING A 900 NUMBER

The sales promotion examples we have given thus far involve the use of an 800 number, the cost paid by the marketer. Now we're going to talk about the use of the 900 number. For using this number the cost is paid by the consumer. The flat cost for use of the 900 number by the consumer is 50 cents for the first minute and 35 cents for each additional minute. The total cost for the marketer is $250, as long as the sponsor maintains a daily minimum of 2,000 calls. Let's look at applications.

Repositioning

How a product or service is positioned in the marketplace often determines the degree of success of the marketer. Positioning, for example, may be for teens, or swinging singles, or newly married, or senior citizens. Positioning might be for specific income brackets, or life style, or taste preferences.

Often repositioning is called for when a brand has a small market share in their present positioning. 7-Up's "Un-Cola" campaign is a

FREE
SATIN™ CIGARETTES AND POUCH.

Offer expires 6 P.M. April 19, 1983.
Only one phone call per household.
Callers must be 21 years of age or older.
Spoil yourself with Satin...on us.

CALL 1-800-554-1300 AND SPOIL YOURSELF WITH SATIN.™

(TOLL FREE. ASK FOR OPERATOR 4.)

Warning: The Surgeon General Has Determined That Cigarette Smoking Is Dangerous to Your Health.

10 mg. "tar", 0.9 mg. nicotine av. per cigarette by FTC method.

Exhibit 5.4.

97

prime example of repositioning. They were positioned against market leaders such as Coke and Pepsi with little chance to gain a major market share. So they repositioned themselves as the "un-cola drink," thus removing their competitive disadvantage and establishing their own unique position.

Such repositioning is not too unusual, but repositioning a TV personality is. Here is how RCA Records used 900 service to help reposition Rick Springfield, who was known for his role on TV's, "General Hospital" where his appeal was primarily to housewives.

RCA Records' objective was to reposition him as a recording star, again appealing to a female audience, but those under eighteen years of age. RCA invited the target audience to call 900-210-RICK to hear an outtake of his latest recording— "Affair of the Heart" from the album "Living in Oz."

This was a sampling technique combined with a contest. When the audience would call, they heard an outtake of the music for about the first thirty seconds. Rick did a voiceover on the music advising of his current concert tour schedule.

During the last thirty seconds, an announcer advised the listener of the contest where there was an opportunity to accompany Rick on his Australian concert tour by simply completing the last verse of his song, "Affair of the Heart." To find out what the other verses were, the listener had to acquire the album because the verses were printed on an in-pack page.

An alternative means of entry was to simply send a self-addressed, stamped envelope, with no need to purchase the record. RCA offered to send the verses of the song.

Results

Some 1.5 million people responded to this campaign, paying the cost of the 900 number phone call. Nobody opted to send in the self-addressed envelope.

Polling

One of the very first applications of the 900 number was for recording votes in polls. For example, during a Reagan-Carter debate in the 1980 election campaign the public was invited to use a 900 number to cast a vote for either Jimmy Carter or Ronald Reagan, indicating which candidate they felt won the debate. Over 750,000 calls were registered, each caller spending 50 cents to cast their vote.

Seeing the responsiveness of the public to the 900 number concept, the broadcast industry has been quick to use the device. Two examples will suffice.

The first example is from "NBC Friday Night Videos." The concept here was quite simple: Call one of two 900 numbers and vote for the rock video of your choice.

When this program aired originally, NBC was receiving approximately 100,000 responses during the 1½ hour telecast. After about the eighth week of programming, the call volume had curtailed and they added an incentive: Call, vote for the rock group of your choice, and you might win a Friday Night Videos T-Shirt. Overnight, response went from an average of 71,000 calls to approximately 175,000. During the sixteen weeks of the telecast, the response increased to a high of over 450,000 responses during one of the ninety-minute telecasts.

The second example involves the tremendously popular program "Saturday Night Live." In one of their most hilarious skits, they tied 900 service into their program. As a result, they accomplished a TV producer's dream: *retaining the viewer audience throughout the time period.*

The key character in the skit was a cook who was about to toss Larry-the-Lobster into a boiling kettle. But the determined cook was restrained until the viewer audience could decide the lobster's fate.

The Larry-the-Lobster skit was in the opening segment of "Saturday Night Live." The audience was asked to vote via 900 number on the question "Should Larry live or die?" with a promise that a preliminary report would be given at the half-hour point. At the half-way point, Larry was actually in danger of facing the death penalty. But as the sixty-minute deadline came, an avalanche of votes from soft-hearted viewers saved Larry-the-Lobster from the boiling kettle.

How many viewers voted for or against Larry? Using 900 service in only two time zones, "Saturday Night Live" received almost one-half million phone calls during their one-hour telecast. Involvement with the audience was the key.

GETTING THE PROSPECT INVOLVED

In each of the examples of sales promotion, we have seen there is a common thread: *getting the prospect involved by telephone.* The kids calling the pirate LaFoote, adults scrutinizing a bottle of Johnnie Walker Red to determine where it is bottled, retail liquor store owners talking to

Gordon's Gin about profit potential, Lee Hill getting senior marketing executives involved in a contest leading to qualified leads, Dr Pepper increasing brand awareness by phone, Coors beer increasing the sale of posters with an 800 number as an ordering device.

And we even saw how tremendous call volume can be created when inviting consumers to call a 900 number at their expense. All of these examples, we believe, provide positive evidence that telephone involvement speeds the process of creating immediate sales or accelerates the decision-making process.

CHAPTER 6

Telemarketing in the Selling Process

"All men are created equal." That's what the Constitution states. Flat out. No "ifs," "ands," or "buts." But...in the business world let's face it—all customers are not created equal. No ifs, ands, or buts about that either.

THE 80/20 PHENOMENON

"Eighty percent of our business comes from 20% of our customers" is a frequent statement at any sales convention. There's hardly a sales executive who isn't aware of the 80/20 phenomenon. Yet—it's quite amazing—we see scores of marketers ignoring it when it comes to allocating advertising and sales dollars, spending the same on all accounts—regardless of potential. Kind of crazy.

This ill-conceived expenditure of effort and dollars is compounded further when marketers likewise ignore the 80/20 principle in lead generation, regarding all leads to be of equal value. They're not.

The telemarketing approach to lead generation and customer activation takes full cognizance of the immutable law—*all prospects and customers are not created equal.*

SELLING TIME

Where salespeople are concerned, time is money. Where and how they spend their time is directly related to how much money they make. **101**

It is startling to learn that time management people estimate that the average outside salesperson spends less than 50% of available time in actual face-to-face selling. (See Table 6.1.)

Table 6.1

Selling	40%
Travel	24%
Waiting	16%
Paperwork and Meetings	20%

Telemarketing, practiced smartly, increases the percentage of face-to-face selling time. And it improves the selling efficiency of salespeople to boot.

THE MAJOR TELEMARKETING APPLICATIONS

There are four major Telemarketing applications that dovetail nicely with the desirable goals of more face-to-face selling time and more selling efficiency.

Table 6.2

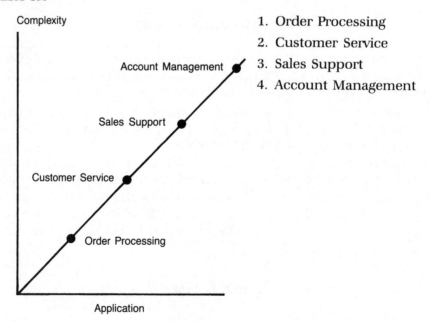

1. Order Processing
2. Customer Service
3. Sales Support
4. Account Management

Applications number one, two, and three relate directly to increasing selling time and sales force efficiency. Application number four—

account management—takes on the complete selling process without the use of an outside sales force.

Inherent in the first three applications is the opportunity to reduce paperwork time on the part of the sales force. Meeting time is repulsive enough to most sales stars. But paperwork—ugh! The very traits that make up superstars are the antithesis of deskbound activities, mixing about as well as oil and water.

It is so much more efficient to turn every possible scrap of paperwork over to "inside people," people who have the training and systems that make them efficient. The time and money saved is enormous, and customer service is improved greatly because a knowledgeable person with current information is readily available when needed.

Order Processing

Order processing is the least complex of Telemarketing applications, yet it is among the most important. A large body of salespeople want to be very much involved in order processing for "their accounts"—from writing up the order to following the order through the production process. This is a natural desire, but more often than not it is counterproductive.

Order-processing people are on the scene at all times. They are trained to write orders properly, schedule production, track orders through the plant or warehouse, schedule shipments in the most efficient manner, keep on top of shipping schedules, and track shipments to destination. That's their job. The job of the salesforce is to *sell*.

Consider these typical dialogues between order-processing people and customers. The customer relations value quickly becomes self-evident.

> "Mr. Mosley—Jay Stewart here. I'm processing the order you gave our representative Bill Quigley yesterday. It's great to have you as a customer.
>
> "I just want you to know we've scheduled shipment for the 16th via UPS with delivery due to arrive at your dock by 4:00 P.M. on the 18th. Yes—that's the fastest and cheapest way. I'll call you at 4:30 P.M. on the 18th to make certain everything is okay.
>
> "Again, it's great to have you as a customer. I'll tell Bill Quigley we talked."

Conversations like these make very favorable impressions on customers—particularly new customers. The telephone contact reassures the customer that the right decision was made in doing business with Bill Quigley and his company. And the customer knows going in that there is a friend in court.

But, the realities of life being what they are, the best laid plans sometimes go astray. And that's where order-processing people pay real dividends.

It's now the 18th—the day Jay Stewart established as delivery date for Mr. Mosley. He makes the call at 4:30 P.M.—the appointed hour. And this phone conversation takes place.

> "Mr. Mosley—this is Jay Stewart. How are you? —Good. Did UPS come through for us? —Good.
>
> "You've got a problem? —One carton was damaged? Oh-oh. I'll get right on it. First thing I'm going to do is send a replacement today by Federal Express. Yes, you'll have it by 9:00 A.M. tomorrow morning.
>
> "Next thing I'm going to do is file a claim for you. No reason you should take the time to do this. Sorry this happened—we'll make everything right. Your business is important to us.
>
> "By the way, call me anytime at our toll-free number—1 800-643-8100. Thanks, Mr. Mosley. I'll let Bill Quigley know we've taken care of this."

Of course, order-processing phone conversations go two ways: to the customer and from the customer. The most satisfying phone call to an order-processing department goes along these lines: "Bill, our word processing department is jammed. We've got a manuscript that's got to be put through in two days. We've got the people, but we need two extra machines. Can you help?" "Hold on." "Jack, we'll have two more machines in your office tomorrow morning." "Great!"

Customer Service

Once friendly contacts are established between order-processing people and customers, Telemarketing can be expanded to a somewhat more complex application: customer service. The customer contacts for this application can often be handled by a senior order-processing person or a more sales-oriented person.

Consider these dialogs as examples of applications by customer service people.

> "Mr. Mosley—just received your latest order. I just thought I'd call you before processing it to point out that if you increase your order

from 120 units to 144 we can give you our gross price, saving you another 10 percent.

"Fine—I'll increase the order. I'll let Bill Quigley know. Thanks."

Customer service in this simple act has (1) saved money for the customer, (2) increased sales and profits for the company, and (3) increased sales and income for the salesperson, Bill Quigley.

Another way customer service people can increase sales and profits is by *cross-selling*. The following dialogue demonstrates this technique.

"Mr. Phillips, we just received your order for 21 Baldwin Cooke Executive Planners and we thank you. You'll have them for your executives well before the first of the year.

"But before writing up your order, I'd like to make a suggestion which I believe will appeal to you. Did you know that we have companion desk planners for secretaries?...Yes, we do. They're called Secretarial Planners and they match the format of the Executive Planner exactly.

"With the secretary and the executive working with the same desk planner format, there is the utmost efficiency. The cost?...Well, if you add 21 Secretarial Planners to your order, you get an extra 5 percent discount.

"Fine. —I'll add the Secretarial Planners to your order. Thank you."

This cross-sell application illustrates nicely the potential for increased sales through the efficient customer service telephone operation.

But let's now look into an application that is likely to occur frequently: customer service during periods in which territorial salespeople are distant from customers within their territory.

Depending upon the type of business, it isn't unusual for a salesperson to cover four or five states. A space representative for a trade publication, for example, might be assigned to five central states such as Illinois, Indiana, Wisconsin, Michigan, and Ohio. The very size of such a territory might dictate that three calls a year per customer is sufficient. Telemarketing can fill the void between calls, providing a good measure of the type of customer service the space representative would provide if it were possible to be on the scene at the appropriate time.

Or consider the situation as it relates to salespeople in the industrial field where large territories and infrequent customer contact are not unusual. Let's listen in on Jay Stewart performing a customer service function with Jim Mosley, Bill Quigley's customer.

> "Hi, Jim. This is Jay Stewart. Bill Quigley is in Dayton this week. But he points out, according to your usage, that you're probably running low on acetone. Our computer printout shows you've been using ten drums a month. On that basis, you'd be down to two drums.
>
> "Sure, why don't you check and I'll phone you at 9:30 tomorrow morning. That way, if you want us to ship you another ten drums I'll have them on a truck for you by 4:00 P.M. tomorrow, giving you overnight delivery. Thanks, Jim."

A dialogue such as this might well prevent losing a customer to competition whose salesperson just happened to be "at the right place at the right time." But such customer-saving and sales-building exercises don't happen by accident. Such events occur only with (1) the utmost cooperation between the sales staff and customer service, and (2) a database that alerts Telemarketing to phone with appropriate information at the appropriate time.

Never to be overlooked is the opportunity for an efficient customer service department to clear up misunderstandings. The words "There's something wrong with the bill I just got" tossed at a salesperson 500 miles from the home office leads to time-consuming phone calls, chances of miscommunication and, very often, a most unhappy customer. That same call, handled by customer service, can most often be expedited quickly and efficiently.

Sales Support

Moving up the scale of applications and complexity, Telemarketing can be key as a sales support function. Applications abound. Here are major applications to contemplate:

- Lead generation (see "Lead Generation Programs," page 109)
- Consumer information line (covered in Chapter 2, "The GE Answer Center"™)
- Scheduling calls for the sales force
- Checking credit
- Followup of proposals submitted by the sales force

- To sell peripheral equipment and supplies that are too small or unimportant for a field salesperson to handle. (An example would be IBM selling computer supplies, typewriter ribbons, etc., through their IBM Direct operation.)

- Dealer contacts to promote use of advertising allowances to promote sale of statement stuffers, package inserts and advertising specialties

- Dealer contacts to check inventory levels and to promote display usage

Each of these major applications is integral to the total selling process. But Telemarketing sales support goes beyond these applications.

Consider if you will, these two opportunities.

- To blitz the customer base with a Telemarketing close-out offer
- To blitz the customer base with a Telemarketing special holiday offer

A Telemarketing sales support staff has another capability that is seldom utilized. The capability to service "orphan accounts"—accounts not currently being served by a sales representative.

Typically when a territory becomes void of sales representation, existing accounts become orphans until a new representative appears on the scene. That need not be. Interim servicing of orphan accounts by the Telemarketing sales support staff can be very effective in maintaining relationships until a territory has new representation.

While the goodwill value of Telemarketing applications to order processing, customer service, and sales support is self-evident, prudence dictates that the economics of special customer service must be considered. Fortunately, the economics of Telemarketing are quite favorable.

An efficient Telemarketing person can support anywhere from five to ten field salespeople. This estimate is based upon the fact that a field salesperson averages anywhere from five to a normal maximum of eight sales contacts per day whereas a Telemarketing person can contact anywhere from twenty-five to fifty or more customers a day. When a marketer computes the additional face-to-face selling time that results and the additional time freed for concentration on A rated customers the potential becomes very exciting.

Account Management

Account management—initiating and completing all sales trans-actions by telephone—is the ultimate in the fine art of Telemarketing. Under this application, *Telemarketing people are the sales force.*

Account management—doing the complete selling job by tele-phone—has developed naturally from the irrefutable law that all customers are not created equal. The cost of sales calls being what they are, there is that group of customers in every customer mix where face-to-face sales calls are not cost-efficient even if a sale is made each time a sales call is made.

We have only to refer back to the A. B. Dick case history in Chapter 1 for a prime example of selling cost exceeding sales revenue. In that example—involving over 100,000 customers—the average cost of an industrial sales call was $66.88; the average revenue was only $50.00. The only alternative to placing this large group of customers into a Telemarketing account mode was "dumping" these customers, leaving them easy prey to competition. A. B. Dick opted for Telemarketing. They won—big.

One of the all-American success stories in the greeting card field is Hallmark Cards. Their distribution blankets America from small hamlets to major metropolitan centers. Their hallmarks of quality, uniqueness, and variety exemplify their famous slogan— "When you care enough to send the very best…"

Hallmark has a network of more than 20,000 dealers, from the smallest of stores to the largest. Every dealer gets equal attention, but in different ways.

Thousands of the smaller dealers are sold and serviced from the state-of-the-art Telemarketing Center in Kansas City. Working with an incredible computer database, each Telemarketing salesperson knows what each dealer purchased by stock number and when he or she purchased it. This inventory system helps estimate the rate of sale and predicts when reorder time is likely to occur. With a database like this, the Telemarketing specialist speaks with the dealer as effectively as if he or she were conversing across the dealer's counter. It's a remarkable system.

Deciding which accounts should be handled by the Telemarketing Center and which accounts should be handled by the face-to-face sales force is really quite simple. It's a matter of dollars and sense. If the cost of a sales call exceeds average revenue, Telemarketing is the obvious alternative.

The opportunity for Telemarketing account management is not

restricted to firms with sales forces, of course. As a matter of fact, accounts gained via direct marketing methods offer great opportunities for Telemarketing account management. But with an important *difference.*

In the case of salesforce-originated accounts, the *smaller accounts* are likely candidates for Telemarketing; in the case of direct marketing-originated accounts, the *larger, more active accounts* are likely candidates for Telemarketing. This may seem to be an enigma. And it continues to be until one examines the intricacies of mail-order buying habits.

Catalog marketers know, for example, that their best prospects are those who have bought one or more times in a current season and who have spent more than average. These are the customers most susceptible to Telemarketing.

Customer groups who have not purchased for two or more seasons and who have purchased less than average rarely qualify as cost-efficient Telemarketing prospects.

In summation, the application of Telemarketing through account management, when done right, will allow cycling through customers on a regular basis meeting objectives such as:

- Efficient order processing
- Cross-selling new products
- Reactivating inactive accounts
- Replenishing inventories
- Capitalizing upon special offers
- Maintaining dialog with key customers

GETTING NEW CUSTOMERS

The primary objective for every Telemarketing program should be *getting more profitable business from present customers.* It is present customers who are every firm's most priceless asset.

But without a continual infusion of new customers, every business is subject to slow death. Telemarketing fits the new business acquisition process as well as it does the customer activation process.

LEAD GENERATION PROGRAMS

How do smart marketers know who their best prospects are? They know by developing customer profiles. And they promote against this sound principle: *Our best prospects are those with profiles that are the same or similar to those of our best customers.*

In the case of firms engaged in business-to-business marketing, profiles are developed by measuring market *penetration* by SICs (standard industrial classifications). Table 6.3 is organized under the government's standard industrial classifications, which neatly fit all businesses into nine major categories, each divided into hundreds of numerically designated subgroups.

Headings (1) through (3) show the number of names compiled by a particular manufacturer for each major SIC classification, number of customers developed from the prospect list, and percent of customer penetration for each major SIC. On the surface, it appears that the manufacturer is doing great; customer penetration ranges from a low of 22.5% to a high of 62.5%, with an average of 39%.

TABLE 6.3 SIC CLASSIFICATION	1. Names on House Prospect List	2. Customers from Prospect List	3. % of Customer Penetration	4. Untapped Names	5. Penetration of Available Names
Agriculture, Forestry, Fisheries	200	45	22.5%	2,810	1.6%
Mining	40	10	25.0%	465	2.1%
Contractors	2,630	870	33.1%	62,580	1.4%
Manufacturers (All types)	8,525	2,655	31.2%	61,385	4.1%
Transportation, Communication, Public Utilities	1,255	785	62.5%	9,270	7.8%
Rated Wholesalers	4,770	1,920	40.3%	32,810	5.5%
Retailers (All types)	8,695	3,130	36.1%	209,705	1.5%
Rated Finance, Insurance, Real Estate	5,410	2,945	54.4%	53,150	5.2%
Rated Service Companies	2,715	1,235	45.5%	83,990	2.6%
TOTALS	34,240	13,595	39.0%	454,780	3.5%

But headings (4) and (5) give dramatic proof that the surface has hardly been scratched. There's 39% penetration of the house list (the list of names compiled by the manufacturer). But penetration of total available like names is only 3.5%. The house-list quantity comes to 34,240. The total of available untapped names in the SIC classifications comes to 454,780—an untapped gold mine of 420,540 names.

Table 6.3 underscores our thesis that all prospects and customers are not the same but it doesn't go deep enough. Who is to say, for example, that all prospects within the SIC categories of agriculture, mining, and contractors are of equal potential? They're not. Table 6.4, which breaks out contractors by credit rating, proves this point conclusively.

TABLE 6.4 CREDIT RATING	1.Names on House Prospect List	2. Customers from Prospect List	3. % of Customer Penetration	4. Untapped Names	5. Penetration of available Names
Listed, but not rated	885	355	40.0%	20,135	1.8%
Not listed	315	65	26.4%	17,465	.4%
Under $5M	40	-	-	4,720	.0%
$5M to $10M	80	15	18.7%	5,885	.3%
$10M to $20M	145	30	20.7%	5,100	.6%
$20M to $35M	110	10	9.1%	2,835	.4%
$35M to $75M	305	135	44.2%	3,405	4.0%
$75M to $200M	240	120	50.0%	1,410	8.5%
$200M to $500M	350	75	21.4%	1,080	6.9%
$500M and over	160	65	40.6%	545	11.9%
TOTALS	2,630	870	33.1%	62,580	1.4%

Applying the maxim that best opportunity always lies with categories having the highest penetration, note the wide range of penetration of available names (column 5) measured by credit rating—from nothing to 11.9%. This revelation gives a clear message: *Concentrate promotion for a lead generation program to contractors against firms rated $35,000 and over.*

Marketers follow an entirely different procedure for developing customer profiles of consumers. For consumer customers, they measure *demographics* and *life styles.* Demographics include age, education, income, marital status, number of children, home ownership, locale. Life styles include sports, hobbies, reading habits, travel habits. The penetration measurements are different, but the marketing principle is the same: Determine who your best customers are and promote to those with like or similar profiles.

Whether a firm is engaged in business-to-business marketing or marketing to the consumer, it all starts with identifying your best customers and therefore your best prospects. No lead generation program—industrial or consumer—can be cost-efficient without this knowledge.

Promotion Strategy Impacts Lead Quality

Of course, even when you have clearly identified your best prospects the quality of leads you will get from your target list will vary tremendously, depending upon promotion strategy. Marketers engaged in lead generation programs classify leads into two broad categories: loose leads and tight leads. Loose leads are generally defined as leads generated as a result of giving a modicum of information about a given proposition, with an attractive reward for responding. Tight leads are generally defined as leads generated as a result of giving a great deal of information about a given proposition with a small reward or no reward at all for responding.

Two things can be predicted with near certainty: (1) a loose lead proposition will produce a higher percent of response, regardless of media, and (2) a tight lead proposition will produce a lower response but a higher percentage of sales closures, regardless of media. The tighter the lead, the more qualified the prospect: the looser the lead, the less qualified the prospect.

It is easy to visualize the impact promotion strategy has on lead quality by comparing two columns with basic propositions stated in two different ways.

Tendency Toward Tight Leads	*Tendency Toward Loose Leads*
1. "Send for our free booklet. We'll have our salesperson deliver it."	"Send for our free booklet. No salesperson will call."
2. "Send $2.00 for this valuable booklet."	"This valuable booklet normally sells for $2.00, but it is yours FREE."
3. "Answer the 10 questions in the enclosed questionnaire and we will send full information."	"Just initial the enclosed card and return. We'll send full information."
4. "Place a stamp on the enclosed card and mail today."	"Mail the postage-free card today."
5. "Agree to a demonstration and we'll give you a valuable booklet that will help you to evaluate your needs."	"Agree to a demonstration and we'll give you a $19.95 pocket calculator absolutely FREE."
6. "Request information on your company letterhead."	"Return the postage-free card today."

The curse of loose leads is that they can have a devastating effect upon a sales force. There's a story of the dictating machine manufacturer who offered to give a stylish umbrella to any executive who requested a demonstration. Leads rained down on them. Most of the leads were returned to the regional offices with cryptic notes such as "I drove 60 miles to follow up this lead. After cooling my heels for an hour, this guy told the receptionist to have me leave the umbrella with her. Don't send me any more of these leads. They're no damn good!"

Lead Qualification

Loose leads or tight leads—the quality will vary within either type. And this is where Telemarketing can play a key role—qualifying the prospect by phone.

At the AT&T National Sales Center (Chapter 3), there is continuous testing of the lead qualification process. They have found sketching prospect profiles to be the most effective process. They ask such questions as:

- How many locations does the caller's company have?
- What is the company's annual sales volume, its cumulative growth record?
- Does the company have any expansion plans?
- How much does the company spend annually on long-distance telephone service?

The answers to questions such as these give a clear profile of the prospect. And matching the prospect profile against the *ideal* customer profile tells the telephone communicator exactly how to rate the lead potential as well as what action to take.

The most efficient way to sort leads is by degrees of potential. Here is how one very successful marketer grades leads by potential. And the disposition taken for each grade.

Code	Grading	Disposition
A	High Potential	Refer to sales force
B	Medium Potential	Sell by telephone
C	Low Potential	Resurface at later date
D	No Potential	Acknowledge by mail

The grading system recognizes that all prospects are not equal. And the action taken is consistent with the potential. It's the neat and efficient way to go.

But the big pay-off is that the sales force gets only leads with high potential. (They don't deliver free umbrellas.) Sales closures go up. Cost of sales goes down.

Lead-flow Monitoring

Qualifying leads via Telemarketing methods is the first step in a successful lead generation program. The second step is monitoring lead flow. Monitoring lead flow is key to maximizing conversion of inquiries to sales.

In the ideal world, the number of inquiries received each day should be equal to the number of leads that can be processed by the Telemarketing Center each day. That's utopia. In the real world, processing all leads while they are "hot"—within 24 hours—is rarely possible. But there are safeguards that can be taken that will guarantee that leads will always be current.

Let's start with the example of a firm that has 22 district sales offices. They employ a total of 175 salespeople. Each salesperson can call upon one qualified sales prospect a day. (The balance of their time is devoted to calling on present customers.) The Telemarketing Center historically qualifies 20% of all leads for processing by the sales force. (The balance are processed by phone and mail.) And the advertising department historically gets a 5% response to their lead generation mailings (see Table 6.5).

With this simple charting method, lead flow is controlled in relation to manpower availability. Lead swamping is eliminated; lead short falls are avoided.

In the AT&T National Sales Center (Chapter 3), lead-flow monitoring is controlled with computer programming. Mailings are released in stages in accordance with expected response and lead requirments. Lead response is measured daily against projected response for each mailing list: twenty or more lists may be in use at any one time.

If the computer says, in effect, "This list will produce 12,651 leads instead of the 12,130 leads you projected," mailings are stopped until telephone communicators can catch up with the leadflow. If the computer says, "This list will produce 9,802 leads instead of the 12,130 leads you projected," more mailings are released immediately. Ah, the computer—it's so smart!

The computer knows, for example, that every lead generation mailing has a lifespan. The computer knows that with the rarest of exceptions: (1) 7% of response will come in the first week, (2) 50% of total

Table 6.5

District Offices	Number of Salespeople in Each	Total Qualified Calls Needed Each Month	Total Leads Required (at 20% Qualified)	Mailings Required (at 5% Return)
Indiana	10	200	1,000	20,000
Tennessee	14	280	1,400	28,000
Virginia	10	200	1,000	20,000
Michigan	10	200	1,000	20,000
Illinois	16	320	1,600	32,000
West Virginia	13	260	1,300	26,000
New Jersey	5	100	500	10,000
San Francisco	8	160	800	16,000
Maine	9	180	900	18,000
Seattle	9	180	900	18,000
New York City	10	200	1,000	20,000
Ohio	10	200	1,000	20,000
Texas	7	140	700	14,000
Utah	3	60	300	6,000
Connecticut	6	120	600	12,000
Pittsburgh	9	180	900	18,000
Philadelphia	11	220	1,100	22,000
Miami	3	60	300	6,000
Des Moines	7	140	700	14,000
Los Angeles	2	40	200	4,000
Denver	2	40	200	4,000
Atlanta	3	60	300	6,000
Totals	175	3,540	17,700	354,000

response in the first four weeks, and (3) the balance of total response over the next six weeks. This illustration shows the response curve.

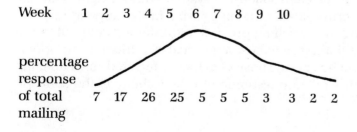

Week   1 2 3 4 5   6 7 8 9 10

percentage
response
of total   7 17 26 25 5 5 5 3 3 2 2
mailing

Lead-flow History

The Telemarketing way of screening leads and the systemized manner of disposing of them leads to a lead-flow history. If history follows the norm about 20% of the leads will be worthy of sales force handling: about 80% will be handled by telephone, put aside for resurfacing at a later date, or disposed of by mail.

But does our interest in these leads end with original disposition? Absolutely not! Out of 1,000 leads, for example, our pictorial history might look like this.

Type	Quantity	Grading	Disposition	Results	Unsold Quantity
A	200	High Potential	Called on by sales force	Sold 35%	130
B	500	Medium Potential	Phone Sales attempt	Sold 20%	400
C	200	Low Potential	Postponed action	None	200
D	100	No Potential	Acknowledged by mail	None	100
	1,000				830

In this example, the sales force brought in 70 new customers and the Telemarketing Sales Center brought in 100 new customers. Nice going. But what about the 130 the sales force didn't sell, the 400 the Telemarketing Sales Center didn't sell, and the 200 low potential prospects tagged for postponed action? Are these all dead? No way!

The reasons for not buying now are legend. "Not ready." "Out of budget." "It's in the hands of a committee." "Your price is too high." "Just shopping." "Satisfied with our present source." Many of the reasons given are "put-offs"; many of the reasons given are legitimate. Put-offs or legitimate, reasons for not completing an immediate sale should be captured and be made a part of the database (see Chapter 8).

Assessing the residue and capturing the follow-up data are critical to maximizing a lead generation program. And let's face it, there's no way to maintain an efficient follow-up system without tight controls. Controls require forms (see Call Report Forms in the Appendix).

Telemarketing in the selling process, from mining gold out of the customer base to finding new customers just like them, is an opportunity open to all of business. Those who have integrated Telemarketing into their marketing mix are testimony to the viability of the concept.

CHAPTER 7

Telemarketing in the Fund-raising Process

"Jim, we need your help...("*Oh, oh—here it comes*")...for a very important cause." "Yes, Governor (or Senator, or Mr. Big, or friend Bill), what can I do for you?" Moments later, like it or not, you are serving on a fund-raising committee. Is there a business executive or active layperson who, one time or another, isn't asked to serve on a committee to help raise funds for a worthy cause?

It's the American way. We raise money for good causes as does no other nation in the world. Each year, hundreds and hundreds of millions are raised for trade associations, labor unions, alumni associations, fraternal organizations, church groups, medical groups, and political organizations. Estimates are that well over $40 billion is raised each year for philanthropic organizations alone.

As staggering as the total contribution figure is, it's a sad fact that most fund-raising efforts are inept in the hands of well-intended amateurs. Remember the venerable Father Devitt whom we met in Chapter 1? He had to raise $20,000 in a hurry to fix a "busted" furnace. And it was only through the wisdom of one of his church members, who recommended a telephone campaign, that the day was saved. Telemarketing techniques are saving the day for scores of fund-raising programs—big and small—across the nation these days.

117

FUND-RAISING BASICS

Mention the telephone in conjunction with fund-raising and the Jerry Lewis Telethon immediately comes to mind. Visions of top performers appear. We see the camera panning a huge bank of volunteers taking pledges by phone as the tote board moves up, up, and up toward Jerry's goal for muscular dystrophy. The telethon is entertaining, exciting, fascinating. It's show biz applied to fund-raising. Millions are pledged by phone each year.

But few, if any, of us will ever be engaged in telethons. We're more likely to be engaged in fund-raising efforts of a more traditional nature and of smaller magnitude. So it is appropriate that we review the basics of fund-raising in the context of which we are most likely to be involved.

The classic way to raise funds for a worthy cause is to take a three-step approach.

1. Form a committee of influentials with the charge to make face-to-face contacts with potential large contributors, establishing a targeted contribution amount for each potential donor.

2. Mount a direct-mail campaign to an identified prospect list (database) of potential contributors.

3. Organize a telephone campaign either in support of the direct-mail campaign and/or to those who have not responded to the direct-mail campaign.

This is the classic three-step approach, but a few other basic facts are in order, as well.

1. Direct mail is now the primary fund-raising method used by nonprofit organizations, accounting for about one-third of all dollars contributed.

2. The highest percent of response in a fund-raising effort comes from previous contributors.

3. The cost of direct mail in ratio to dollars raised can range from a very low percentage—3% to 5%, for example—for mailings to a select list of previous donors to 100% and more for mailings to people who have never contributed before.

4. Favorable response to telephone solicitations usually can be enhanced when calls are made by people of stature in a community, or in an industry.

5. It generally is agreed that people respond best to emotional appeals, backed by *rationale* for giving.

6. People tend to respond more readily to appeals for specific projects rather than for general needs. Example: "Will you help us to raise $92,000 so we can give Braille books to the blind?"

7. When pledges are made by telephone, it can be expected that 75 to 80% of the pledges will be collected, if properly followed up.

8. When a telephone campaign is done properly to selected lists, the pledge rate can be as much as ten to twelve times that of direct mail.

9. The average contribution tends to increase when specific contribution amounts are suggested. Example: "You contributed $20 last year. May we suggest you contribute $25 this year to help our expanded needs."

10. Total amount pledged tends to be greater when a multipayment plan is offered.

11. Setting a specific date for meeting a fund-raising goal tends to increase response and total contributions.

FUND-RAISING PRINCIPLES APPLIED

More often than not, business executives get involved in a fund-raising program when their trade association identifies a worthy industry effort for which funds are required over and above funds normally generated from members.

Such was the case a few years ago with the Direct Mail/Marketing Educational Foundation. Annual income from members covered the cost of bringing college students—all expenses paid—to the Lewis Kleid Institute twice each year. But the foundation had a much larger goal: to establish direct marketing degree programs at three major universities.

For this goal, the foundation had no funds. And it was calculated that it would be necessary to raise a capital fund of $1.2 million to underwrite the program. A tremendous task.

How did the foundation organize to reach their ambitious goal? They followed the classic three-step approach.

1. They formed a committee of influentials to make person-to-person approaches with major organizations having a vested interest in

direct marketing, organizations capable of pledging $15,000 to
$30,000 and more over three years.

2. They developed a mailing package to go to the 2,400 members of
   the Direct Marketing Association, all of whom also had a vested
   interest in the future of direct marketing.

3. They made arrangements with CCI, a leading Telemarketing
   agency, to phone all members who did not pledge as a result of
   person-to-person contact, or as a result of the direct-mail effort.

The letter—a five-pager, plus pledge card—follows (Exhibit 7.1).
Much of the story behind the fund-raising effort is told in the letter, as
you will see.

STONE & ADLER INC.

150 NORTH WACKER DRIVE
CHICAGO, ILLINOIS 60606
(312) 346-6100

June 1st, 1982

Mr. Jerry Greenberg
The Finals
149 Mercer Street
New York, New York 10012

Dear Mr. Greenberg,

Remember when you were a kid. A "dreamer" was put down
as someone who would never amount to anything—destined
to be a "non-achiever" for life.

What a myth!

Let me tell you about some "dreamers" who became super
achievers in direct marketing. They succeeded beyond
their wildest dreams.

There's the thrilling story of L. L. Bean in Maine. For
years they ran a successful mail order business...catering
to outdoorsmen.

But Leon Gorman dreamed of new horizons...a new world out
there of men and women who never fished or hunted—dressed

Exhibit 7.1.

the way outdoors people dress. A pipe dream? Hardly, Leon
Gorman turned dream to reality. Sales—plateaued at the
$50 million level—boomed past the $100 million level in a
few short years.

What about the legendary "kitchen table" people? Len
Carlson, out in California, is a part of the legend.

Len and his wife Gloria shared a dream. They dreamed they
could put together a catalog of hard-to-find gadgets that
would appeal to the masses. Thus Sunset House was born.

Fifteen years and a customer base of 6.5 million names
later, the press announced Sunset House had been acquired
by a major corporation for a price reported to be in the
millions.

The most remarkable dream story on the agency side is that
of Lester Wunderman. Les was an account person with the
Max Sackheim agency. He dreamed of having his own agency.

But an agency that would apply sophisticated direct response
techniques to all media—including a "new" medium called
television. Today his firm—Wunderman, Ricotta & Kline—
has billings in excess of $100 million, with offices in New
York and 12 foreign countries.

As you read of these dreams-come-true I hope you are recall-
ing your own. The dreams you have had which have helped you
to get to where you are today.

> But of all the dreams-come-true which I have
> witnessed over the years there is one which
> supersedes all others. A dream-come-true
> which has touched all our lives, a dream
> which will live on beyond our lifetimes.

The year was 1965. Lewis Kleid, a leading list broker in
his day, was a close friend of Edward N. Mayer, Jr., known
around the world as "Mr. Direct Mail."

Lew made a proposition to Ed. He said, "Ed—if you will
devote time to teaching the rudiments of direct marketing to
college kids, I'll provide the seed money to make it happen."

Exhibit 7.1., continued

Thus, with the simplicity that was a trademark of Ed Mayer,
the Lewis Kleid Institute was launched. Today, almost 17
years later, The Direct Mail/Marketing Educational
Foundation, a non-profit organization which sponsors Kleid
Institutes, continues in the Ed Mayer image.

> Over the past 17 years over 1,000 bright college
> students have taken the 5-day intensive course,
> sponsored by the Foundation ...all expenses paid.
> It is estimated that over 50% of these students
> have entered into a direct marketing career.

As one of the privileged few who has had the honor of lectur-
ing each new group of candidates over many years—I only
wish you could witness, as I have, the excitement that comes
to each as they are introduced to the wonders of direct
marketing disciplines.

"I learned more in five days than in my four years as a
marketing major," is a somewhat typical statement from one
of these exuberant students.

But let me give you just a few quotes from hundreds in file.

"I learned so very much—the week just set my spark for
direct marketing into a big roaring fire!"

> Marilee Gibson
> Yorchak
> New Mexico State
> University

"The Institute has greatly increased my awareness and understanding of direct marketing, and furthered my career interest."

> Tim Harrison
> University of North
> Carolina

"If one of your objectives was to stimulate young, ambitious
people to enter your field, you succeeded with me."

> Paula Miante
> College of William and
> Mary

Exhibit 7.1., continued

I guess from all of this one would have to conclude our dream has truly come true. Well—not exactly.

None of us ever dreamed that direct marketing would have the explosive growth we have all experienced. (As an aside—when I wrote my first book I trumpeted that total sales of goods and services via the direct marketing method had reached the staggering figure of $300 million. The estimated figure for 1981 is $120 *billion!*)

So now we realize that if our true dream is to be realized—growing our own at the college level to people our future growth—we are going to have to raise our sights beyond the far horizon.

Where we are bringing the gifted student to the Institute—only one each from about 35 colleges twice each year—we've got to get Direct Marketing taught on the college campus in full semester courses. Not to three score and ten for five days. Instead—to hundreds for full semesters.

Is this "The Impossible Dream"? No!

I'm going to tell you about what some regard to be an emerging "miracle," which is in the process of happening as I pen this letter.

At a Board of Directors meeting a few months ago in the offices of The Direct Mail/Marketing Educational Foundation, Richard L. Montesi, President, made a startling proposal. A proposal which he stated would make our ultimate dream come true.

The ultimate dream, as he expresed it, is to establish a Chair for a Direct Marketing Center in three major universities: one in the Middle West; one in the East; and one in the West.

The full-scale curriculums will be structured to earn a degree in Direct Marketing for each graduate, carrying with them a stature similar to that enjoyed by a graduate from the Wharton School of Business or Harvard Business School.

"An exciting idea," we said. "But how are we going to fund these centers?" "From a capital fund of $1.2 million," Dick said. "$1.2 million. Good God!" was the reaction.

Exhibit 7.1., continued

Well then the miracle started happening. Andy Andrews, one
of the directors, said—"Why don't we go around the table
right now and see how much commitment we can get over the
next three years from the small group of directors at this
table?"

Would you believe we raised $120,000.00—10% of our goal—
within five minutes!

When we left that day a few of us agreed to write some
letters and make some phone calls. And what happened as
a result surpasses anything in my experience.

Remember those "dreamers" I talked about earlier? Well let
me tell you what happened with some of them.

Remember Leon Gorman of L. L. Bean? He's committed $15,000
over three years. And Len Carlson—another $15,000. And
Les Wunderman—$15,000. They're putting their money where
their dreams are.

The list goes on. "Dusty" Loo of Looart Press—a major
commitment. John Flieder of Allstate Insurance—"Count
us in." Kiplinger Washington Editors. The Kleid Company.
Jim Kobs of Kobs & Brady—"Absolutely!" Publishers
Clearing House. Grolier. Colonial Penn. Rodale Press.
Spiegel. American Express.

John Yeck of Yeck Brothers Group—"You can count on us."
Eddie Bauer. Rapp & Collins. Ogilvy & Mather. Alan Drey.
The DR Group. Hanover House. And on and on.

> To this moment, these people and some others we
> have contacted bring total commitments to
> $725,000. So we have reached 60% of our goal!

This is exciting in itself, but equally exciting is the
fact that we have two formal proposals from two major
universities detailing how a Chair would be established
for Direct Marketing. And the cost.

One proposal is from UMKC—University of Missouri, where
Martin Baier of Old American has taught Direct Marketing
classes for a number of years. The other proposal is from
New York University. Both universities are ready when we are.

Exhibit 7.1., continued

So we are this close to bringing off a 20th Century miracle!

Now we come to you to ask you to share in this dream of dreams. There is a pledge card inside of the enclosed enve- lope. The amount suggested is just that. A suggestion. You are the best judge of what your company should pledge against the future.

I have asked for and have gotten approval to have your response come back to me personally. I'd like to hear from you even if there is some unforeseen circumstance under which you cannot make a pledge.

We must decide very soon upon the first university to establish a Direct Marketing Center. Therefore I will appreciate it if you will reply within the next 10 days. Thank you so very much.

Sincerely,

Bob Stone

P.S. It is my fondest dream that you and I will be there to witness the commencement exercises of the first graduating class with a degree in Direct Marketing.

"A Margin of Excellence"

THE DIRECT MAIL/MARKETING EDUCATIONAL FOUNDATION
CAPITAL FUND RAISING PROGRAM

Our organization wishes to participate in the DMMEF Capital Fund Raising Program. Our 3-YEAR PLEDGE is indicated to the right.

Contribution Category	Payment Schedule
☐ Leadership Gift $10,000 annually $_____	payable by July 15, 1982
☐ Major Gift $5,000 annually $_____	payable by 1983
☐ Special Gift $2,500 annually $_____	payable by 1984
☐ Supporting Gift $1,000 annually	

Company _____

Officer Name _____

Address _____

Signature _____

Pledges are for three years only and are nonbind- ing commitments. Reminders will be mailed thirty days prior to the payment dates indicated above.

YOUR TAX DEDUCTIBLE GIFT WILL MAKE A DIFFERENCE

Exhibit 7.1., continued

A couple of comments about the letter and pledge card before we talk about the telephone campaign: First, most neophytes would be aghast at a five-page letter, but the fact is that no letter is too long if written to the interest of the reader.

Second, the letter encouraged pledges by telling what the reader's peer group had already pledged, confirming the acceptance of the worthy goal. And finally, the letter had a sense of urgency— "We must decide very soon upon the first university to establish a Direct Marketing Center."

The pledge card employed two fund-raising principles: (1) pledges will be larger if you spread them over time (three years in this case), and (2) suggesting a specific amount (amounts suggested were in ratio to the dues a member paid) improves the chances of a pledge in that amount.

The mailing package was a huge success. Only a handful of those who responded favorably pledged less than the requested amount. But the foundation was still short of their goal. And this is where Telemarketing techniques put the campaign over the top.

The Telemarketing Program

The strategy for the telephone effort was developed by the late Murray Roman, founder of Campaign Communications Institute, a pioneer in Telemarketing. He first reviewed the membership prospect list, eliminating those who had already pledged, and then selected from those remaining the ones he considered most likely for telephone solicitation.

This list agreed upon, he then prepared a script for a taped message from Bob DeLay, president of the Direct Marketing Association, and Bob Stone, chairman of Stone & Adler, Inc. The taping completed, his agency started making calls within a few days.

The procedure was for the CCI telephone communicator to ask the prospect permission to play a taped message from Bob DeLay and Bob Stone. The taped message follows.

BOB DELAY: This is Bob DeLay. I am asking that you take a few minutes to hear Bob Stone and me talk about an industry opportunity that depends so much on your good will and support. We are talking to you on tape via telephone to be sure you personally get our message and because we like to reach our members as quickly as possible while there is still time for decision making. But here is Bob Stone to tell you more about that opportunity.

BOB STONE: Thanks, Bob. I really appreciate your kindness in allowing me time to bring you up to date on the progress that has been made in the Educational Foundation fund-raising drive. One word that I think describes the progress best is *terrific!*

It's amazing to me that in the most trying of times direct marketers of all sizes across the nation have responded so favorably. This has convinced me that our objective of growing our own talent is absolutely right. I have seen many pledges come through for $15,000; many for $7,500 and scores for $3,000. On the other hand, one company contributed $30,000 and another $52,000.

These major contributions are great but some of the smaller pledges have thrilled me the most. One was from a 24-year old by the name of Michael Gersen who said, "At age 24, recently experiencing the lack of specialization in our university system, I feel your dreams and the steps you have taken are of the utmost importance. I am not in a position to commit an annual gift, however, I would very much like to show my support with the enclosed contribution." And enclosed was his personal check in the amount of $50.00. Isn't that great?

So here's where we are at this point in time. We are approaching the $900,000 mark with a little over $300,000 to go. To fall short of our goal now, to fail to educate the talent we will need in the future would be tragic.

As I said in my letter to you, the amount of the pledge suggested was just that—a suggestion. I am going to ask the telephone communicator to repeat the suggested pledge for you in a moment.

Let me say, whatever amount you consider adequate from your standpoint will be a profitable investment in the future. And what a great day it will be for you and me and everyone else in direct marketing when we see bright young talent graduating with B.A.s and MBAs in direct marketing. Then our futures will indeed be secure. Thank you for listening.

Upon completing the playing of the taped message, the CCI telephone communicator came back on the line and asked for a three-year pledge in the exact amount suggested in the mailing piece. Results were astounding: 18% of those called made a pledge. The campaign went over the top.

So here is a classic example of putting the three-step approach into practice. The person-to-person phase raised $725,000; the direct mail/telephone phase raised $505,000. Grand total: $1,230,000—all from 2,400 prospects!

APPLICATIONS FOR PHILANTHROPIC ORGANIZATIONS

Much can be learned about the application of Telemarketing techniques to fund-raising by studying how philanthropic organizations use the phone. Our case study for this purpose involves one of the most prestigious institutions of its kind—Memorial Sloan-Kettering Cancer Center, first established in 1884.

The annual operating budget for the center is large—almost $250 million. The report for a recent twelve-month period reveals a break-out of sources of operating income and categories of operating expenses.

Operating Support

Patient Care Revenue	$171,627,000
Government Agencies	39,445,000
Voluntary Agencies	3,411,000
Philanthropic and Other Restricted Funds Applied	16,580,000
Other	4,614,000
Total Operating Support	$235,677,000

Operating Expenses

Salary and Payroll Costs	$171,967,000
Supplies and Other Costs	66,763,00
Depreciation and Interest Expense	10,629,000
Total Operating Expenses	$249,359,000
Net Operating Loss	$(13,682,000)

The net operating loss is offset annually by unrestricted philanthropy and income from investments. Continual fund-raising is essential to meeting the budget.

Speaking with Glen Bonderenko, direct mail manager, we learned that direct mail is a major part of the center's fund-raising efforts. The Memorial Sloan-Kettering Cancer Center has a list of 260,000 active donors—those who have contributed one or more times over the past three years. Active donors are solicited eight times a year for additional donations. In addition, Mr. Bonderenko's department mails approximately 5½ million pieces of mail each year soliciting new donors (see Exhibit 7.2). "We set high standards in the selection of our direct-mail copy," says Mr. Bonderenko, "and we only use an approach that reflects this. We have discontinued appeals that are not consonant with our standards." Such are the ethical concerns of Memorial Sloan-Kettering.

May 29, 1984

Mr. John J. Jones
123 Main Street
Anywhere, U.S.A. 00001

Dear Mr. Jones,

I'm writing to you today to explain why the on-going cancer research at Memorial Sloan-Kettering is so important to you: Last year an estimated 2,100 people died of lung cancer in Wisconsin.

Perhaps someone you know—a loved one or a friend—has lung cancer. It's quite possible, because this disease is the most common form of cancer, and one of the most difficult to control.

And unfortunately, the incidence of lung cancer is on the rise for both smokers and non-smokers alike.

Right now there are only three ways of treating cancer—surgery, treatment using anti-cancer drugs, or radiation.

But some cancers—like lung cancer—do not respond well to existing forms of treatment. And because of this we must find new and different approaches for treating these difficult cancers. This is our goal, and we need your support to reach it.

Because research efforts are so important, I want to ask you to consider making a generous gift of $25, $50, or $100 to enable us to continue our vital work.

Exhibit 7.2.

We also need major tax-deductible gifts of $1,000...even $5,000 or more.

You see, there are so many potential areas of research. So many new approaches we must try. But for that, we need sufficient funds.

One promising approach is to try to make a diseased cell reverse its cancerous growth and return to its original normal function.

I know this may be difficult to envision, but it has been done in the research laboratory.

In recent laboratory experiments conducted here at Memorial Sloan-Kettering, we were able to reverse the abnormal growth of cancer cells in mice.

This exciting finding may eventually offer hope to people with inoperable cancer, as well as cancer in any form.

Of course, this research is still in its earliest experimental stages, and it is only one of many research projects currently underway here. But important advances are being made.

For example, after years of research, scientists here at Memorial Sloan-Kettering were able to synthesize an antiviral drug called FIAC. This is a major advance in cancer treatment because so many cancer patients die from viral infections after being weakened by chemotherapy.

Your support helps make this type of valuable research possible. This is why I urge you to support Memorial Sloan-Kettering Cancer Center in our efforts to find new ways to control cancer.

I hope you will decide to make a generous gift to support on-going cancer research at Memorial Sloan-Kettering. For the sake of your loved ones and thousands of potential cancer victims, I can't think of a more important decision you could make.

Sincerely,

Mortimer H. Chute, Jr.
Vice President for Development

Exhibit 7.2., continued

Memorial Sloan-Kettering Cancer Center

Make the decision to help... Your gift will continue the vital cancer research currently underway at Memorial Sloan-Kettering Cancer Center.

Enclosed is my gift of: ☐ $25   ☐ $50   ☐ $100   ☐ $____

```
Mr. John J. Jones
123 Main Street
Anywhere, U.S.A. 00001

                                            ZB3M4
```

Please return this card with your tax deductible gift to:
Memorial Sloan-Kettering Cancer Center, Sort 8918, New York, NY 10043

Exhibit 7.2, continued.

Testing Telemarketing

In 1982, Memorial Sloan-Kettering Cancer Center, not unlike other philanthropic organizations, started to feel the impact of a reduction in federal funding. This triggered a need to raise additional funds through another medium. And Telemarketing was the logical medium to test.

The Test Universe:

Working with Institutional Development Counsel, a professional fund-raising organization, a test model was developed. There were 2,350 prospects selected for the test: 1,106 new donors and 1,244 lapsed donors. After eliminating prospects without phone numbers and those considered special or major prospects, 1,426 prospects remained. Lapsed donors selected were those who have given $50 to $499 as their largest gift. New donors selected were those who had given $25 or more.

Promotion Strategy:

Promotion strategy involved three elements.

1. A one-page pre-approach letter mailed to all prospects over the signature of John Miltner, director of development at the time, thanking the prospect for the most recent gift and alerting them to a forthcoming "important letter."

2. A second letter mailed to prospects one week after the first. This three-page letter was signed by the eminent Paul A. Marks, M.D.,

president of Memorial Sloan-Kettering Cancer Center. The letter alerted the prospect to the phone call they would be receiving in a few days, and asked that the prospect consider a specific amount, based upon the prospect's giving history.

3. Ten days to two weeks later, the prospect was approached by telephone and asked for a pledge commitment. In phone conversations, prospects were urged to make multipayment pledges over time.

Results:

By any fund-raising standard the test was successful. As the overall results disclose, actual cost-per-dollar raised came to 25 cents.

Number of Prospects	1,426	
Prospects Not Called	343	
Prospects Called	1,083	
No Decision—Specials*	90	43 Special*
		47 Call Back
Prospect Decisions	993	
No Pledge	722	(72%)
Pledges	271	(28%)
Average Pledge	$277	

Projected Budget for Test	$9,820
Projected "Goal" For Test	$51,700
Projected Cost-per-Dollar Pledged	$0.19
Actual Cost of Phone/Mail Test	$12,504
Actual Dollars Pledged	$76,202
Actual Dollars Received	$49,877
Actual Average Gift	$184
Actual Cost-per-Dollar Raised	$0.25

*A "special" is defined as a prospect that could not be reached by telephone (i.e., on vacation, number changed to an unlisted number, deceased, etc.).

More detailed analysis of the 28% who pledged brought revealing facts to light—each fact a fund-raising basic. Analysis showed, for example, that the propensity to pledge had a direct relationship to the recency of the last gift.

Year of Last Gift	% Who Pledged
1981	56%
1980	Not selected for calling
1979	25%
1978	16%
1977	1%
1976	2%
	100%

Analysis of the effect of emphasis on multipayment pledges over one payment gifts is also revealing. Only 39% were multipayment pledges as contrasted to 61% one payment gifts. But 51% of total dollars pledged came from the multipayment pledge group, again proving the maxim, "Total amount pledged tends to be greater when a multipayment plan is offered."

One successful test deserves another. And Glen Bonderenko has continued the testing procedure in a methodical way. Strategy for the first test called for two pre-approach letters prior to the phone call: strategy for the most recent test called for no pre-approach letter.

For the most current test, two groups were selected: "actives" who had contributed $50 to $499 and "inactives" who contributed $100 to $4,999. A telephone script was prepared as a guide for telephone solicitors to use in approaching each group. The script for inactives follows.

Hello, may I speak with Mr./Mrs./Ms._____? Good morning/ afternoon/evening Mr./Mrs./Ms._____. This is_____. I am calling for Memorial Sloan-Kettering Cancer Center in New York. How are you?

(Pause)

In (year) you sent a generous gift of $_____to support our cancer research efforts. Thank you for your support.

Mr./Mrs./Ms._____we need your help again. Federal funding is declining and the support of our friends has helped us continue vital research which otherwise would have ended.

And this is why we are asking you to renew your support this year.

Would you consider increasing your gift to $_____?

(If no) Well, perhaps you would renew your previous gift of $_____?

(*If still no*) What amount would you like to send?

(*If already given*) I'm sorry—I'll check our records and make sure this is corrected.

(*Confirmation*)

Fine, thank you so much. I'll be sending you an envelope to mail your gift in.

Please let me check your address ...

Again, thank you for your time and support, Mr./Mrs./Ms_____.

The script for Active donors is more aggressive, as you will see.

Hello, may I speak with Mr./Mrs./Ms_____? Good morning/afternoon/evening Mr./Mrs./Ms_____. This is _____. I am calling for Memorial Sloan-Kettering Cancer Center in New York. How are you?

I'd like to thank you for the generous gift you gave us last year of $_____.

Because of the wonderful support of people like you, funding for our research programs has remained firm at a time when federal funding throughout the country has been declining. This vital research is bringing us closer to ultimately controlling and curing cancer.

While federal grants will continue to be a major source of research funding, private support from friends like you Mr./Mrs./Ms_____ will have to increase if we are to maintain the quality of our research.

This is why we are counting on your support again this year. Would you consider increasing your gift to $_____?

(*If no*) Well, perhaps you would renew your previous gift of $_____?

(*If still no*) What amount would you like to send?

(*If already given*) I am sorry. I'll check our records and make sure they are corrected.

(*Confirmation*)

Fine Mr./Mrs./Ms_____. Thank you so much.

I'll be sending you an envelope to mail your gift in. Please let me check your address....

Again, thank you for your time and your support, Mr./Mrs./
Ms_____.

Results Achieved:

Once again, active donors responded more favorably: 45.7% to
16.3% for inactives. But the average gift from inactives—those who
previously contributed $100 to $4,999—was higher than actives—those
who had previously contributed $50 to $499, higher by 35%. And this
proves another maxim: *Donors tend to set the amount of a current gift by
what they contributed previously.* So inactives who previously contributed larger amounts are indeed worth pursuing.

But the bottom line of the most recent test showed a cost-per-
dollar raised of 38 cents contrasted to a cost of 25 cents per dollar raised
for the first test. Conclusion: Pre-approach letters and multipayment
pledges pay for Memorial Sloan-Kettering Cancer Center.

Fund-raising—it will always be with us. Done right, with Telemarketing as its ally, it can serve to help achieve the goals of more and
more worthy causes.

CHAPTER 8

Developing and Maintaining a Database

Knows name of daughter, when she got married, what her husband does, where she lives. Knows name of wife, knows her extracurricular activity. Knows the type of coat pockets Martin prefers, the fact he needs a handkerchief pocket that will accommodate a second set of glasses, knows that the front and back of trousers have to be let out, knows he likes a vest with adjustable strap, knows he likes lightweight wool suits for winter, knows what he bought last, knows he likes thin pin stripes, knows the shade of blue he likes, knows his size. And the piece de resistance: Willie knows that if he can get Dorothy to come in with Martin his sale is almost assured because this is exactly the type of suit Dorothy likes on Martin.

The above paragraph is by way of reintroduction of the lovable Willie Potts of Jack Henry, whom you met in the first chapter. Willie learned long ago that the more you know about your customer—buying habits, preferences, personal likes and dislikes, background, affiliations, and so on—the better the chance of maintaining a macro-customer relationship.

Willie's database system is, to a major degree, instinctive. And it's manual. But the principles he applies are found in the most sophisticated computerized databases, computerized systems with the added inherent advantage of being able to manipulate thousands of bits of data—all to the benefit of the marketer.

GATHERING MEANINGFUL DATA

It is the gathering of meaningful, manipulative data that is the key to a successful database management program. For Jack Henry, the men's store, meaningful data is quite different than for a steel supply company, for example.

The database requirement varies greatly by category of business, to be sure. But for the Telemarketer, regardless of category of business, there is a guideline to follow that should lead to a meaningful database. Ask this question: "What data will I need on my CRT (cathode ray tube) in order to carry on a meaningful conversation with the customer?

For Telemarketers, a key source of data is the call report. The call report should capture the history of each account and give direction for future servicing. Basic data, which should go into the database, includes the following:

- Key contact
- Title
- Telephone number
- Best calling time
- Time zone
- Mailing and shipping address
- SIC # (standard industrial classification)
- Source of original contact
- History of purchases
- Current buying pattern
- Special requirements
- Credit limit
- Personal notes
- Other products/services in the discussion stage
- Log of calls by dates
- Follow-up call cycle

With this data safely stored in the computer, carrying on meaningful dialogues with a customer base becomes a piece of cake. The computer makes sure that each telephone salesperson is given a list of scheduled follow-up calls each day. Prior to each call the total picture of the account appears on the screen. Complete recall results. Even though a salesperson might have a block of 400 accounts, he or she can be as knowledgeable in conversation with a given account as if the salesperson had none other to serve.

GATHERING SOURCE DATA

The value of providing telephone salespeople with customer data is self-evident. But database management goes much deeper than that. It starts with measuring the efficiency of advertising and promotion, knowing which publications, which mailing lists are cost efficient from a customer acquisition standpoint. Throwing all leads into a pot, regardless of source, is the way it was done in the dark ages. With database management, you know which publications are cost efficient, and which aren't.

Let's say you are mounting a lead generation program. You decide to use six different mailing lists. By tracking sources for each, you might come up with a table that would look something like this.

Table 8.1   Lead Generation Program (Direct Mail)

List	Quantity Mailed	Total List	% of Response	% Sold	Average Order
A	5,000	24,000	5.0%	10%	$300.00
B	5,000	30,000	2.5%	20%	340.00
C	5,000	50,000	10.0%	2%	120.00
D	5,000	40,000	3.5%	6%	350.00
E	5,000	40,000	5.0%	5%	300.00
F	5,000	15,000	6.0%	10%	280.00
Averages	5,000	199,000 (Total)	5.33%	8.9%	$281.66

If we throw everything into the pot, we find that our lead generation mailing averages a response of 5.33%, that we sell an average of 8.9%, and that our average order comes to $281.66. But those are *averages*. By tracking each source, we quickly discover we have at least one "dog."

List C, front-end, looks great: 10% in inquiries—the best response. But look at the back-end: only 2% sold and an average order of only $120.00. With no back-end tracking, the marketer would most certainly have mailed the balance of 50,000 names on List C. Not only would this pull down average percentage sold and average order, but it would have devastated the telephone salespeople handling the low quality leads from this list source.

Now let us say that we decide upon a continuation mailing to all the lists with the exception of List C and that we get the same type of response. Table 8.2 shows the picture.

Table 8.2   Continuation Mailing for Lead Generation Program

List	Mailing Quantity	Response	% Sold	No. of Sales	Average Order	Total Sales
A	19,000	5.0%	10.0%	95	$300	$ 28,500
B	25,000	2.5%	20.0%	125	340	42,500
D	35,000	3.5%	6.0%	73	350	25,500
E	35,000	5.0%	5.0%	87	300	26,100
F	10,000	6.0%	10.0%	60	280	16,800
	(T)124,000 (A)4.4%		(A)10 .0% (T)440		(A)$314	(T)$139,450

T—Total: A—Average

Our percent and number of leads is down. But our closure rate and average order—the two factors that count—are up. And let us not overlook the money saved in the Telemarketing program by not processing poor quality leads, plus the money saved by not mailing 45,000 pieces to List C. Only by tracking responses by sources and putting this information in your database is it possible to know which mailing lists and which publications lead to the best end result.

Tables 8.1 and 8.2 deal specifically with getting new customers—first orders. Once a prospect becomes a customer, it's important that the original source of inquiry be carried right into the *customer database.*

Lists A and B, for example, look extremely good with closure rates of 10 and 20%, respectively. But the true test is, how well do these customers perform after the first order? By punching the original source into the customer database, the answer to this all-important question can be called up any time. And what the computer tells you is often a shocker.

MANIPULATING DATABASES

"I've got tons of information in my database, but I don't know what to do with it" is an often-heard complaint, but not so with the major catalog firms. Not only do they know what to do with their data, but they know how to manipulate it to maximize profit.

The concept of manipulating customer data came about almost out of sheer desperation during the Great Depression. Catalog giants like Sears and Wards were feeling the impact of bread lines, as were all businesses. Working against the maxim that "All customers are not created equal," they developed a formula that changed the way mail-order customers were promoted. And this formula, with refinements, is being used to this day.

The R-F-M Formula

This magic formula was tagged as R-F-M (recency, frequency, monetary). Best customers, and therefore those most likely to buy again, were identified as those who had bought most recently, those who bought most frequently within a specified period, and those who had spent specified amounts.

Through testing, the mail-order giants learned that these three criteria—recency, frequency, monetary—were the basis for maximizing profits. Indeed, they soon found it possible to develop pro-forma statements that enabled them to predict with deadly accuracy what their profits would be based upon which customers they selected to receive their current catalog and which customers they excluded from their current circulation.

In its simplest form, the R-F-M formula calls for a point system to be established with purchases broken down by quarter of the year. A typical formula might be as follows:

Recency points:

24 points—current quarter

12 points—last six months

6 points—last nine months

3 points—last twelve months

Frequency points: Number of purchases × 4 points

Monetary points: 10% of dollar purchase with a ceiling of 9 points. (The ceiling avoids distortion by an unusually large purchase.)

Number of points allotted varies among those using R-F-M formulas, but the principle is the same. Once the system is established and point values are assigned, the opportunities for maximizing profits are almost phenomenal. I've seen sophisticated systems that have scores of categories with profit figures ranging from $50 per thousand catalogs mailed to $1,500 and more. Under the system, each account is isolated from all other accounts. Buying habits dictate how frequently an account is solicited.

Once the R-F-M system is computer programmed, producing a monthly update is a simple matter. Table 8.3 shows what a hypothetical partial printout might look like for a representative group of accounts. The table shows the activity of five accounts for December 1984. Account number 16,441 bought twice in September and once in December. Recency points were computed in relation to the time interval since each purchase.

Table 8.3   Analysis of accounts by recency, frequency, monetary—December 1984

Account Number	Month	Recency Points	No. of Purchases	Frequency Points	Dollar Purchases	Monetary Points	Total Points	Cumulative Total Points
16,441	9	12	2	8	32.17	3.21	23	39
16,441	12	24	1	4	46.10	4.61	32	71
16,521	1	3	3	12	87.09	8.71	23	23
16,608	7	12	1	4	21.00	2.10	18	28
16,708	4	6	1	4	33.60	3.36	13	18
16,708	8	12	2	8	71.00	7.10	27	45
16,708	11	24	1	4	206.00	9.00	37	82
16,921								68

Frequency points were computed by multiplying the number of purchases by four. Monetary points were computed by multiplying the dollar amount of purchases by 10%. Note that under "Cumulative Total Points" this marketer had carried over sixteen accumulated points from the previous calendar year, indicating that his customer first bought in calendar year 1983.

In reviewing the list of accounts, note that account number 16,708 spent $206 in November but was given only nine monetary points. This reflects the arbitrary decision of the marketer to give no more than nine monetary points regardless of amount of purchase. Finally, note that account number 16,921 shows no activity for calendar year 1984 but has a total of 68 points for 1983.

The opportunities for manipulating a data base under the R-F-M system are immense. And, of course, the system need not be restricted to catalog firms. It is clearly applicable to Telemarketing.

The R-F-M System Expanded

Robert Kestnbaum, a noted authority on database management, has altered and added to the R-F-M formula. He has found for his clients—those engaged in direct marketing and Telemarketing as well—that profits are maximized even further by employing his altered formula, which goes under the acronym FRAT.

F stands for frequency of purchase within a specified period. (Kestnbaum gives the greatest weight to frequency.) He follows this factor with recency of purchase. Then amount of purchase, followed by type of merchandise, or service, purchased. The T is an important addition to the R-F-M formula, for what a person buys currently serves as a statement about what else that person is likely to buy in the future. For example, subsequent purchases of a woman who just bought support hose are likely to be quite different from the woman who just bought jogging shoes.

Given a database that provides almost unlimited manipulation fires the flames of imagination. Think of the commands that can be made of the computer on behalf of a Telemarketing Center.

- "Give me a list of all our customers who have bought two or more times in the last six months."

- "Give me a list of all our customers who first bought within the last three months."

- "I want all the names of those who bought Product X in the last 12 months so we can phone them about preference treatment in testing our new model."

- "Let me have a list of everyone who bought a personal computer from us in the last year. I want to mount a phone campaign to sell our new software program."

If you've got the database, the computer will give you whatever you ask for. Fast.

Cross-Selling

Our exploration of database manipulation continues.

One of the most exciting potentials is in the area of cross-selling. When you know what every customer buys it's a simple matter to cross-sell related products.

Consider banks, for example. The computer can easily segment out all accounts by class and dollar amounts.

Savings Accounts	Commercial Real Estate Loans
Personal Checking Accounts	Inventory Loans
Commercial Checking Accounts	Accounts Receivable Loans

Money Market Checking Accounts	Car Loans
Home Mortgages	Home Improvement Loans

Pinpointing accounts by class and amount leads to cross-selling opportunities. Commercial checking accounts, for example, are prime prospects for inventory loans. Savings accounts are prime prospects for car loans. Those who have paid down, or paid off home mortgages are prime prospects for equity loans. Opportunities for cross-selling abound.

Major insurance firms have mastered cross-selling. And they have the databases to make it happen. They know all about their policy-holders: ages, home ownership, marital status, children and their ages. And they know which policies each policyholder has with the company.

These insurance companies can get a printout any time they want of all policyholders turning age 65, say within six months. Their cross-selling opportunity in this instance would be supplemental medicare insurance.

These insurance companies can get a printout any time they want of families with pre-school children. The cross-sell opportunity in this instance would be an educational insurance program.

The database manipulation opportunities are practically endless. Cross-sell hospital insurance to accident insurance policyholders. Cross-sell cancer insurance to hospital insurance policyholders. Cross-sell homeowner's insurance to mortgage insurance policyholders. And on and on.

The Rule of Two

One of the most overlooked opportunities in Telemarketing is the potential for improving the odds that a new customer will order a second time and therefore will become an active customer.

We know of a catalog firm in Wisconsin—Lands' End—that works on the principle that the first order they receive from a prospect is a *trial:* Customer status is established only with the second order. (Thus the expression "the rule of two.")

When a prospect orders from Lands' End for the first time, he or she is likely to get a surprise phone call. The dialogue is along these lines: "Good morning, I'm Mrs._____ of Lands' End. We appreciate your business and I'm calling to ask if you are satisfied with your purchase. I'll be your service representative. So please phone me any time I can help at our toll-free number—1-800---------."

The wisdom of this investment in new customers—establishing a warm, caring one-on-one relationship at the outset—is borne out by drop-off figures between the first and second orders in industry after industry.

One example will illustrate the point. A firm selling Christmas gift items to business firms charted their repeat business percentages for a period of eleven years, starting with the second year. Their percentages looked like this.

Year	% of Repeat
2	34.2
3	60.0
4	71.2
5	75.9
6	76.0
7	79.3
8	79.9
9	80.9
10	79.8
11	77.8
12	83.8

What this chart disclosed was that this Christmas gift marketer ended up with 342 repeat buyers the second year for every 1,000 new customers they put on the first year.

But as we study percentages for subsequent years we note that of those who remained after the second year 60% repeated in the third year until in the twelfth year 83.8% of the residue were repeating. So clearly the second year was the critical year. Getting that second order opened the opportunity to get high repeat percentages in subsequent years.

Having clearly identified the critical year, this marketer launched an intensive Telemarketing campaign against this key segment of their customer base. The campaign was a huge success: Second-year buyer percentage increased by a whopping 16%. The rule of two—Telemarketing can make it happen.

OTHER DATABASE APPLICATIONS

Companies who have mastered the techniques of database management are profiting from the use of their databases in their

Telemarketing Centers. Note these applications for three diverse business categories.

Mail Order

Fingerhut, a $400 million plus company out of St. Cloud, Minnesota, sells the gamut from hard goods to soft goods, home furnishings, apparel, leisure equipment and auto accessories—all via direct marketing.

Fingerhut began its Telemarketing program in 1979 when it saw the need to clarify missing information on incoming mail orders. "What we were looking for," says Steve Leighton, director of sales, Fingerhut Marketing Services, "is the response from the customer at an acceptable cost per order."

One of the first things Fingerhut learned was that Telemarketing could expedite order processing and improve service to the customer in general. But that wasn't all they learned.

"We quickly learned," Steve Leighton says, "that once we had the customer on the phone, we had another opportunity to sell additional merchandise."

Referring to their database, Leighton notes, "In our St. Cloud operation we are tied into a computer. We call up the customer's order on the screen and phone. The customer is contacted on the basis of the products ordered. We look for a particular order or particular product and try to do what we call an add-on order. In other words, we're increasing sales with a related or complementary product to the original purchase."

Airlines

Without a doubt, the most sophisticated database system in the airline industry is the one developed and maintained by American Airlines. At an investment in excess of $130 million, no less!

Back in the 1970s, American made an indepth study of where their business was coming from. While they were servicing some 25 million passengers annually, they found that a major share of their business—perhaps as much as 65%—was coming from a relatively small number of individuals, about 800,000 or so who were averaging thirteen trips a year on American.

Digging deeper into statistics on target markets, American Airlines found that just as relatively few frequent travelers make up the large body of total passengers, so do a relatively small number of travel agencies—about 7,000 in all—accounting for the lion's share of their travel agency business. This small group accounts for almost 35% of American's total annual revenue.

Target markets identified, American proceeded to develop what later became known as the Sabre System. Referring to the system, Mr. R. L. Crandall, president and chief operating officer of American Airlines, said, "The Sabre System has enabled American to automate such diverse functions as tickets and boarding passes, crew scheduling, baggage tracking and our direct marketing program."

Sabre video display units have been installed in most all the targeted travel agencies. "A travel agent sitting at a Sabre video display unit has at his or her fingertips a wealth of information and special features with which to respond to a customer's needs," said Mr. Crandall.

"There are more than 2.9 million different airfares in Sabre," he continued, "as well as schedules for more than 125,000 city pairs served by 567 airlines worldwide. Sabre can automatically price—in seconds— nearly 84% of all the itineraries booked through the system," concluded Mr. Crandall.

The Sabre database system has proved invaluable to American's Telemarketing Center. Mr. George Mueller, senior director of passenger sales, relates how Telemarketing was employed to sell a new product called "AAirpass"—long-term transportation. To qualify for an "AAir-pass," a prospect had to make a five-year commitment, fly at least 25,000 miles a year. And—get this—the prospect had to deposit $20,000 cash up front.

The original intention was to use Telemarketing for lead qualification for the field sales team charged with selling "AAirpass." "We were sixty days into the program," said Mr. Mueller, "when we discovered our telephone agents were actually able to sell this product over the phone, not just pre-sell.

"And when we could close sales of $20,000 over the telephone in a service-related industry without a face-to-face sales call, we thought we ought to be able to sell almost anything we have. We went on to prove the system by using Telemarketing to sell our company meeting convention services," concluded George Mueller.

Brokerage Houses

Prudential-Bache might best be described as the new breed of brokerage house. They've gone far beyond traditional trading in stocks and bonds.

Playing off the 80-20 rule—80% of your business coming from 20% of your customers—they have developed a Telemarketing program that caters to the top 20% of their clients, recognizing their choice clients as COMMAND® Account customers.

Andy Varley, senior vice-president of the COMMAND® Client Service Center of Prudential-Bache, explains their Telemarketing program this way: "Our customers are busy, successful people. They can use the 800 number from anywhere in the country and check their account balance, portfolio status, VISA Card charges and balance. They feel comfortable with the COMMAND® concept and that's what's important.

"Without our Telemarketing Center, the COMMAND® Account would not be possible. With a dedicated direct terminal tied to the Prudential-Bache mainframe and customer database, the representative can access all information, money fund balances, checking, and VISA Card information. Each COMMAND® representative takes care of about forty calls a day," Mr. Varley concluded.

Database management and Telemarketing: A great duo.

CHAPTER 9

How to Do Market Research Via Telephone

Market research, in its simplest form, involves asking questions. There is no medium more efficient for this purpose than the telephone. It's quick; it's cost-efficient. You can ask questions as part of any telephone inquiry or order-getting process. Or, you can conduct specific studies—telephone surveys—to concentrate on the questions you use.

RESEARCH OPPORTUNITIES AT POINT OF SALE

Every telephone inquiry or order presents an opportunity to learn something useful about your customers. Consider these examples.

1. "We appreciate your order for 10,000 envelopes, Mr. Jones. May I ask—in the course of business, about how long will this supply last?"

2. "Thank you for your inquiry, Mrs. Sullivan. May I ask—what prompted you to call us?"

3. "We appreciate your catalog order, Mrs. Johnson. Do you have any particular friends whom you believe would also like to receive our catalog?"

4. "We have specials from time to time that we offer to our best customers by phone. What would be a good time to call you? During the day, evening, weekdays, or weekends?"

5. "You have been a loyal catalog customer of ours for a number of years. We want to serve you even better. Are there any other items you would consider buying from us if we carried them?"

6. "We understand, Mr. O'Connel, that your corporation has other branches and we'd sure like to serve them too. Would you be kind enough to give us the names of your counterparts and may we use your name when calling?"

Each example carries with it an opportunity to get useful information. And, it is so easy to do at the point of sale. Let's go back over the six examples and explore their research value.

Example 1: By knowing normal consumption time for each envelope buyer, the manufacturer can punch this information into the computer and phone for reorders prior to depletion time.

Example 2: By tracking sources of inquiries, the marketer can measure advertising efficiency by media. "Saw your commercial on Channel 9." "Read your ad in *Reader's Digest*," etc.

Example 3: The secret of successful catalog marketing is to get more customers just like those you have. By asking customers for names of friends, you are more likely to get the names of the same kind of people.

Example 4: By asking customers the best time to call, you eliminate the hazard of calling at a time that might upset a good customer. Such research data can be put into a database with ease.

Example 5: By compiling a list of other items customers might buy from you through the simple process of asking the question, you develop an opportunity to expand your line.

Example 6: Many manufacturers have many branches. But it is not unusual for a company to be selling only one or two of several branches. The number of branches sold can usually be expanded by enlisting the assistance of a satisfied customer in one of the branches.

These are but a few examples of the opportunities for research at the time of inquiry, or sale. Research questions are a natural extension of a phone dialogue.

It really comes down to asking the right questions: Questions that will help you to serve the customer better; questions that will help you to find more customers just like those you've got.

INTELLIGENCE GATHERING VIA SURVEYS

Sometimes we have more questions than we can include in our ongoing Telemarketing scripts. And often it's important that we separate the selling process from the information-gathering process.

This need for separation is a key consideration. In our surveys, we want our customers (and prospects) to know that we are genuinely interested in what they have to say. They are being asked, in effect, to give us counsel—their honest perceptions, unclouded by a "selling" effort on our part.

So when we have special issues or many questions to examine, it's best to employ the survey approach. And it's best to employ an experienced survey researcher to help.

To get the word, we went to John Eighmey, Ph.D., senior vice-president and director of Account Research Services of Young & Rubicam/New York, one of the world's largest advertising agencies. John Eighmey has conducted research for some of the world's largest advertisers—a great deal of it by phone.

Eighmey regards market research as "intelligence gathering." He tags gathering intelligence by phone as "teleresearch" to distinguish it from Telemarketing.

"Conditions change, customer needs and the ways of satisfying those needs change," stated Dr. Eighmey, "but the principles of successful selling remain. One of those principles—perhaps the most important one—is knowing the territory in which you operate, understanding your customers." He then pointed out that survey research can be a major tool in developing better prospect lists and phone dialogues if we get answers to key questions like these.

1. *What are my best customers like, and why are they my best customers?* Who are they? Where do they work? What do they do? What are their goals—for their companies, for themselves? How do they feel about my products and doing business with me? These are obvious questions, but how good are our answers?

2. *What do my best customers think about my competitors?* What are they buying from my competitors? What do they think of my competitors? How might I be at an advantage, or disadvantage?

3. *What are my customers plans for next year?* What products will they need from me?

4. *What else could I sell to my best customers?* Are they fully aware of my product line? What new products could I develop?

5. *How satisfied are my customers?* What things could I do to improve product quality for my customers? What useful features or services could I offer?

6. *Why have many of my leads not been converted to first-time sales?* What could "rejectors" tell me about what I'm doing wrong, or not doing for them?

7. *Why have so many first-time customers failed to become regular customers?* Did the product they bought fail to "deliver" on expectations? Do my other products fit their interests or needs? Are they even aware of the other things I sell?

8. *Why have many customers become "lapsed" customers?* How did I lose touch with them? Competitor activity? Have their needs changed?

As we review these eight questions—there could be scores more—we can readily see the need for basic research to better understand our customers, what they are doing, what their plans are, and how better to fit in with them. As Dr. Eighmey puts it, "If we can improve our response rates, increase our average order size, or keep competitors away from our best customers, then research can be worth a small fortune." Reflecting on the eight questions, Dr. Eighmey points out that each has two common elements.

1. *A clearly defined group of prospects or customers.* Each question stated or clearly implied a specific group of people we would want to approach. These groups include prospect lists, qualified leads, nonresponding leads (or prospects who rejected us), best customers, first-time (or trial) customers, lapsed customers, infrequent customers, our competitor's customers.

2. *An important and clearly expressed information need.* If members of these groups are contacted, the right questions are properly asked, and the answers are properly analyzed, we will have found ways to get customers and serve them more effectively.

Dealing with these two elements—specific groups of people and specific questions—is a natural for the telephone. "Indeed, one might observe that the use of the telephone for survey research was the precursor of Telemarketing," said Dr. Eighmey. "Both involve contacting clearly defined groups and a dialogue, or a verbal structured question-naire in the case of surveys. In the survey research business, the telephone has become the mainstay for information gathering, replac-ing for the most part expensive personal interviews."

CONDUCTING A TELEPHONE SURVEY

To the uninitiated, conducting a survey by telephone is a scary thought. The idea that the consumer, much less the business executive, will cooperate through a detailed survey is difficult to believe. Yet the professional knows that the preponderance of people do cooperate. There's something flattering about being asked to participate in a survey, even among the most sophisticated.

Another common misconception about surveys is the thought that you have to interview hundreds, even thousands to get valid results. "Not so," says Eighmey. "There is usually no need to interview the vast majority of a large group if scientific methods of selecting a represent-ative number are properly employed." The uncanny accuracy of politi-cal surveys these days among an infinitesimal percentage of the population confirms this statement.

To better understand the approach to and the structure of a telephone survey, we asked Dr. Eighmey to provide us with a real-life example.

The survey that follows was conducted to learn how marketing and advertising decision-makers (particularly executives in major corpora-tions) view direct-response advertising. The sponsor of the study wanted to know the extent to which these executives were aware of the rapid changes taking place in the direct-response industry.

The objective of the survey was to get information that would help the agency in communicating with its clients and with the advertising industry in general. Would top executives see direct-response advertis-ing in a limited fashion (maybe thinking of it only as direct mail) or would they see it as an area of growing options and utilities (including Telemarketing)? That was the question.

The group defined for this survey was marketing and advertising directors in Fortune 500 companies. A sample was drawn from this list, and interviews were completed with 111 executives.

The first step for every call was to identify the correct person to talk with (called "screening of respondents" in the survey research busi-ness). In this case, they dialed the company chairman's office and asked the secretary to identify the director of marketing or, if not available, the director of advertising. And, only one person was interviewed in multidivision companies.

Once the interviewers found the right executive, they were guided by the following questionnaire.

DIRECT RESPONSE METHODS SURVEY

Hello, this is _____, calling for (name of research company) of Princeton, New Jersey. We're conducting a brief survey with senior marketing and advertising executives about direct marketing. Specifically, the survey concerns the kinds of techniques you consider to be direct marketing and the role these techniques play or can play in helping direct marketers understand how their services are thought of by other businessmen.

1. To begin with, we are interested in the kinds of selling techniques you consider to be direct response methods. Which techniques or methods do you consider to be direct response? (PROBE: Any other techniques?) DO NOT READ LIST TO RESPONDENT. RECORD ORDER OF MENTION 1, 2, 3, ETC., IN SPACE PROVIDED.

Q. 1

A. DIRECT MAIL _____

B. TELEPHONE SELLING _____

C. TELEVISION OFFERS _____

D. OFFERS CARRIED THROUGH
   NEWSPAPER ADS _____

E. OFFERS CARRIED THROUGH
   MAGAZINE ADS _____

F. INSERTS IN NEWSPAPERS
   OR MAGAZINES _____

G. OTHER (SPECIFY): _____
   _____
   _____

DON'T KNOW/NONE
MENTIONED   X

2. Now I'm going to read you a list of some direct-response methods some companies use to promote and sell their products. For each one, please tell me if your company is now using the technique. (READ LIST)

	YES	NO	*NOT SURE*
a. Direct mail	1	2	3
b. Telephone selling	1	2	3
c. Television ads with direct response address or phone number	1	2	3
d. Magazine ads with direct response offers other than cents-off coupons	1	2	3
e. Newspapers ads with direct response offers other than cents-off coupons	1	2	3
f. Magazine or newspaper inserts	1	2	3

3. Are there any other direct response methods your company is using?
   1. YES -What are those techniques?

   _____

   _____

   _____

   2. NO -(IF NO DIRECT-RESPONSE METHODS USED ON Q. 2 AND Q. 3, SKIP TO Q. 6)
   3. NOT SURE

4. Here are a few purposes companies sometimes use direct-response methods for. For each one I read, please tell me how useful you think direct-response methods are in your business for achieving each purpose—very useful, somewhat useful, only slightly useful, or not useful at all. First … (READ ITEMS.)

	Very Useful	*Somewhat Useful*	*Slightly Useful*	*Not Useful*	*Don't Know*
a. Lead generation to identify possible prospects for followup sales efforts	1	2	3	4	5

	Very Useful	Somewhat Useful	Slightly Useful	Not Useful	Don't Know
b. Lead qualification to identify the best prospects from a large listing of possible customers	1	2	3	4	5
c. Direct selling or taking orders for your products and services	1	2	3	4	5

5. Which of the following three statements best describes your use of direct-response methods? (READ EACH STATEMENT)
   a. Direct response is the *major way* our company promotes and sells its products.

   or

   b. Direct response is an important part of *a mixture of methods* our company uses to promote and sell its products.

   or

   c. Direct response is only a minor part of *a mixture of methods* our company uses to promote and sell its products.

   GO TO QUESTION 7

ASK THIS QUESTION ONLY IF RESPONDENT DOES NOT USE ANY DIRECT-RESPONSE TECHNIQUES ON Q. 2 AND Q. 3. OTHERWISE SKIP TO QUESTION 7.

6. Do you think any of the direct-response methods I just read you could be used to sell products to your company's customers?
   a. YES—ASK 6A BELOW
   b. NO—SKIP TO 6B BELOW
   c. DON'T KNOW—SKIP TO 6B BELOW

IF "YES," ASK:

6A. What would you say are the major reasons your company isn't now using direct-response methods? (PROBE: Any other reasons?)

IF "NO" OR "DON'T KNOW," ASK:

6B. Why do you say that?

Finally, two questions for background purposes.

9. Does your part of the company sell to consumers, other businesses, or both?
   a. Consumers
   b. Businesses
   c. Both

10. Does your part of the company have or use ...? (READ EACH ITEM).

	Yes	No
a. Television advertising	1	2
b. Newspaper or magazine advertising	1	2
c. Its own field sales force	1	2
d. Manufacturers representatives or other sales agents	1	2
e. Its own local offices or stores for customers	1	2

THANK YOU FOR YOUR HELP!

*TIME FINISHED:*_____

*LENGTH OF INTERVIEW:*_____

The findings were useful and of interest to the readers of this book. For example:

- The responses indicated that half of the senior marketing and advertising executives think of direct mail first when asked to list direct-response methods. The direct-mail legacy is strong; telephone is not top-of-mind (yet).

- It was learned that most executives saw direct-response methods as being a minor part of their mixture of selling programs. Clearly, there is a need to "tell the direct marketing story" and those who understand the story first (and capitalize on it) will realize an important advantage over their competition.

This example was simple and direct. We wanted to show the reader the similarities between the telephone survey questionnaire and Telemarketing scripts.

Often, however, the questionnaires are a little longer and involve more complicated switching among questions. For example, the questions and their sequences often depend on the exact answers given by respondents (these are called "skip patterns").

For these surveys (and even for the simpler ones), we can merge the technologies of the telephone, the computer, and the CRT to make use of the most powerful and efficient information-gathering tool— Automated Telephone Research.

AUTOMATED TELEPHONE RESEARCH

As one might expect, AT&T has taken a leadership position in telephone market research from a technological standpoint. Automation is the key to their telephone interviewing operation at their data collection center in Piscataway, New Jersey. Their center is known as the Telephone Research and Analysis Center (TRAC).

Here are some of the functions of the TRAC system as used for market research purposes:

- *Entering of questionnaire.* Permits simple typing of questionnaire into the CRT. Permits logic and handling options to be entered immediately or after entry of the questionnaire.

- *Skip pattern changes.* During the interview, allows unnecessary questions to be skipped, thus avoiding keeping the respondent on any longer than necessary.

- *Answer consistency check.* Allows for the automatic checking of a previous answer to determine whether or not current answer is consistent with one or more previous answers.

- *Control of calling across time zones.* Allows only telephone numbers in the same time zone to be called if you have a national sample.

- *Display telephone number.* Displays telephone number to be called on screen. (There are even automatic dialers being used in conjunction with this feature.)

- *Interviewer training.* Provides a "subsystem" that allows a new interviewer to be trained on the interviewing system. Provides practice files and prompts instructions.

- *Open end answers.* Allows for recording of verbatim responses, both multiple and single responses. Controls whether answer is multiple or single.

- *Response time.* Has no longer than a half-second delay in questions and answers appearing on the screen once a respondent's answers are entered.

- *Rotation of questions.* Rotates a series of questions to ensure that each question has the same opportunity to be asked at each place in the series and will occupy that place equally with all other questions in the series.

- *Call back control.* Provides for the automatic display of a telephone number for call-back purposes. Allows call-back limits (number of times) to be set, record times, date, and respondent to call back. Displays at appropriate time to effect a timely call back.

- *Summarize supervisory data.* Provides running total/averages, etc., of the following: average time per interview, completes per hour, completes per interviewer—total and by hour, number of busys, terminates, completes, wrong numbers, disconnects, refusals, etc., by interviewer, and total per hour.

- *Monitoring capability.* Allows the monitoring via CRT of any selected interviewing station. The interviewer's action on the terminal will be duplicated in a real time sense on the monitoring terminal. This facilitates training of new interviewers and assures the consistency and reliability of the data that is collected.

- *Management information reporting (Tabulation).* Provides summaries of the responses by key variables such as: age, sex, type of industry, etc. Gives researchers quick access to market data.

In the case of AT&T, the TRAC facility is easily accessible to their marketing units. Product managers can monitor the progress of their projects and get immediate reactions from customers on service offerings or promotional campaigns. Market researchers, working with product managers, can easily revise or add questions.

When the TRAC system is applied by an internal market research department, additional advantages accrue: (1) a company can have better control over the cost of its market research budget, (2) protection of proprietary information, and (3) greater flexibility in the number and types of market research projects.

SOME "RULES OF THE ROAD"

No single chapter of a book can cover all the "how to's" of doing survey research via the telephone. So far, we have taken a look at the important questions we can ask of our customers with answers that will help us become more productive in serving them. We've also looked at an example, and at AT&T's TRAC system.

What follows, then, is a discussion of some rules of the road, things to consider when working with telephone surveys.

1. *What questions do you really want answered?* Just as a Telemarketing script or dialogue follows a chain of logic, so should a good survey questionnaire. This logic chain should center on the issues you want to illuminate. Resist the temptations to ask every co-worker's favorite question, and resist fishing expeditions. This may sound like obvious advice, but the lesson is hard to learn. It is a frequently made mistake.

2. *Phrase questions clearly and without personal bias.* It is almost a "natural fact" of human communication that the questions we ask are either leading or confusing.

- *Leading*—we imply through our question wording the answers we want or expect to hear.

- *Confusing*—we usually use too many words.
  Just as you pretest your Telemarketing scripts or dialogues, you should try out your survey questionnaires. Make sure you are being understood.

3. *Define your "target" carefully.* Each one of the questions posed in the first pages of this chapter centered on a clearly defined customer group and clearly expressed issues of concern for each group. For example:

- Best customers
- First-time customers
- Lapsed customers
  Surveys of customer groups that are not clearly defined tend to produce murky results.

4. *Get a respresentative sample of customers from the customer groups you want to survey.* Use methods of selecting samples for interviewing that give each customer in the group an equal chance of being interviewed. There are many procedures to use, but

whatever you do it should depend on scientific sampling. The survey researchers you work with will know how to do this.

5. *Do not confuse quantity with quality.* Five hundred people well interviewed (important issues thoroughly and carefully questioned) will be more useful than 1,500 people superficially interviewed. Up-front thinking about the logic of the questionnaire is very leverageable time. It should lead you to a questionnaire that produces a greater depth of understanding about what your customers are thinking and doing. And confidence in what you have learned comes as much from the *quality* with which you question individual customers as it does from the *quantity* of customers you contact.

6. *Make sure that you represent yourself, your surveys, and your selling efforts honestly.* Never use the guise of "We are conducting research: Can you answer some questions?" as a foot-in-the-door sales technique. It is bad business. It is also a violation of the FTC Act for which companies have been prosecuted.

- Customers resent this approach when they recognize what is going on.
- It undermines our ability to do research: customers won't know who to trust.
- It will undermine Telemarketing too.

The telephone and market research are natural allies. They work best, however, when you ask the right questions, and when you respect the distinction between information telephone surveys and telephone selling.

CHAPTER 10

The Mathematics of Telemarketing

We've come a long way together since the first chapter of this book. We've explored the major Telemarketing applications in depth.

- Order processing
- Customer service
- Sales support
- Account management
- Sales promotion

We've seen many documented case histories to prove the value of these Telemarketing applications. But as fascinating as the case histories may be, let's face it—each reveals the success of someone else. Not you. The measurement of success of each of us is our own numbers. So in exploring Telemarketing opportunities for ourselves, it behooves each of us to work within a structure that will give us quantitative and qualitative data for the applications we pursue.

USING THE NORMS

The first step in this process, when exploring a new business opportunity, is to look for numbers that might be used as *norms.* To get these norms we went to Rudy Oetting, president of R. H. Oetting & Associates, Inc., a leading Telemarketing agency in New York City.

Inbound/Outbound Costs

There are two sets of numbers that are key to estimating Tele-marketing costs: (1) cost per call for handling *inbound* calls from business firms and consumers, and (2) cost per call per decision-maker contact in making *outbound* calls to business firms and consumers. Mr. Oetting provided the following range of costs for each.

Approximate Inbound Cost per Call

Category	Range of Cost
Business	$2.50 to $5.00
Consumer	$1.50 to $3.00

Approximate Outbound Costs per Decision-Maker Contact

Category	Range of Cost
Business	$6.00 to $10.00
Consumer	$2.50 to $4.00

The difference in cost range between inbound and outbound calls should be explained. In the case of inbound calls, the initiator is always a prospect or customer: The caller phones at a time of his/her convenience with a view to getting further information or negotiating an order. In the case of outbound calls, the initiator is always the marketer: The call may be made at an inconvenient time for the prospect and the caller may have to generate awareness about a new product or service. Consequently, outbound calls are usually of longer duration and often require more experienced, higher paid personnel.

The range of costs, whether for inbound or outbound, depends a great deal upon the Telemarketing application and the complexity involved for each application.

The following table indicates where ranges of costs are most likely to fall, on average, by application.

Application	Low Range	High Range
Order processing	X	
Customer service	X	
Sales support		X
Account management		X
Sales promotion	X	

Developing Worksheets

Knowing the average range of costs for inbound and outbound calls is key, but it is just the start. The operation of an in-house Telemarketing Center requires a full range of personnel. And is subject to taxes, fringe benefit costs, incentive costs, equipment costs and collateral material costs as well. To get a true picture of all monthly costs, worksheets are advised.

Rudy Oetting has provided us with two representative worksheets: one for inbound and one for outbound.

Exhibit 10.1: Inbound—9:00 A.M. to 5:00 P.M.

Exhibit 10.2: Outbound—9:00 A.M. to 5:00 P.M.

EXHIBIT 10.1   Inbound: 9:00 A.M. to 5:00 P.M.

Monthly Expense Statement

Representative Phone Hours (1235) Direct Expenses	Cost	Cost/Phone Hour
A. Labor		
Manager (⅓ time)	$ 1,000	$ .81
Supervisor (full time)	2,500	2.02
Representatives (10 full time)	14,300	11.58
Admin. (2 full time)	1,906	1.54
Tax and fringe (⅓ of wages)	7,062	5.72
Incentive	1,500	1.21
Subtotal	$28,268	$22.88
B. Phone		
Equipment and service	500	.40
Lines:		
• WATS	15,947	12.92
• *MTS (Message Toll Service)*	–	–
Subtotal	$16,447	$13.32
C. Other		
Lists	–	–
Mail/Catalogs	2,470	1.00
Postage	1,235	.50
Miscellaneous	1,000	.81
Subtotal	$ 4,705	$ 2.31
Total Direct	49,420	38.51
G&A (15%)	7,413	5.78
Totals	$56,833	$44.29

Exhibit 10.1.

Basis for Expense Statement: Exhibit 10.1

Labor

Manager:	Annual = $36,000 × ⅓ allocation = $1,000/month
Supervisor:	Annual = $30,000 at full allocation = $2,500/month
Representatives:	$8.25/hour × 40 hours/week × 52 weeks full allocation = $1430/month 6.5 phone hours/day × 19 days/month = 123.5 phone hours/month
Admin:	$5.50/hour × 40 hours/week × 52 weeks full allocation = $953/month
Tax and fringe:	33.3% of wages (including contest incentives)
Incentives:	Reps Only—$1,500/month

Phone

WATS (800) =	*Step Rate 18 plus Band 5 42 minutes (70%) per labor hour WATS Connect Time: 1235 hours × 0.70% = 865 billable WATS hours plus 10 lines @ $36.80/line access

Note

The *average* number of calls handled per rep phone hour is 12 @ 2.3 minutes each. As high as 15 per phone hour during peaks.

Computations:

1. @ 12 calls/hour = $3.69/call   3. @ 1 Order/rep phone hour = $44.29 per order

2. @ 15 calls/hour = $2.95/call   4. @ 6 Order/rep phone hour = $7.38 per order

*Step Rate 18 (Local State) plus Band 5 (all other continental states plus Puerto Rico and Virgin Islands).

Exhibit 10.1., continued

EXHIBIT 10.2   Outbound: 9:00 A.M. to 5:00 P.M.

Monthly Expense Statement

Representatives Phone Hours (1235) Direct Expenses	Cost	Cost/Phone Hour
A. Labor		
Manager (⅓ time)	$ 1,000	$ .81
Supervisor (full time)	2,500	2.02
Representatives (10 full time)	13,000	10.53
Admin. (2 full time)	1,906	1.54
Tax and fringe (⅓ of wages)	9,015	7.30
Incentive	8,667	7.01
Subtotal	$36,088	$29.21
B. Phone		
Equipment and service	350	.28
Lines:		
• WATS	12,729	10.31
• MTS (Message Toll Service)	3,075	2.50
Subtotal	$16,154	$13.09
C. Other		
Lists	3,088	2.50
Mail/Catalogs	617	.50
Postage	309	.25
Miscellaneous	1,235	1.00
Subtotal	$ 5,249	$ 4.25
Total Direct	$57,491	$46.55
G&A (15%)	8,624	6.98
Totals	$66,115	$53.53

Basis for Expense Statement: Exhibit 10.2

Labor

Manager:	Annual = $36,000 × ⅓ allocation = $1,000/ month	
Supervisor:	Annual = $30,000 at full allocation = $2,500/ month	
Representatives:	$7.50/hour × 40 hours/week × 52 weeks full allocation = 1300/month	
	6.5 phone hours/day × 19 days/month = 123.5 phone hours/month	

Exhibit 10.2.

Admin: $5.50/hour × 40 hours/week × 52 weeks at
                           full allocation = $953/month
Tax and fringe: 33.3% of wages (including contest incentives)
Incentive: Reps Only—40% of Total Renumeration

Phone Step Rate 18 plus Band 5*
WATS =   35 minutes (50%) per labor hour WATS connect
                           time:
                           1235 × 50% = 617 billable WATS hours
                           plus 10 lines @ $31.65/line access

MTS (Message Toll Services) =
                           5 minutes per labor hour connect time:
                           1235 × 8.3% = 102.5 Message Toll @
                           0.50 Min. = $3,075

Computations:

1. @ 12 TDs (total dialings) per rep phone hour cost per dial = $4.46
2. @ 15 TDs (total dialings) per rep phone hour cost per dial = $3.57
3. @ 5 DMCs (decision-maker contacts) per phone hour cost per
DMC = $10.71
4. @ 6 DMCs (decision-maker contacts) per phone hour cost per
DMC = $8.92
5. @ 1 Order per rep phone hour cost per order = $55.53
6. @ 3 Orders per rep phone hour cost per order = $17.84

*Step Rate 18 (Local State) plus Band 5 (all other continental states plus Puerto Rico
and Virgin Islands).

Exhibit 10.2., continued

It is easy to see how worksheets lead to capturing all the numbers. The key numbers to explore are (1) cost per phone hour, (2) cost per call, and (3) cost per order (or response). A review of the computations for Exhibit 10.1 (inbound) shows a significant difference in cost, for example, when phone representatives are able to handle fifteen incoming calls per hour as contrasted to twelve calls per phone hour. And the cost per order drops dramatically if the representative is able to close six orders per phone hour, for example, as contrasted to one per phone hour.

Likewise for Exhibit 10.2 (outbound) significant differences are to be noted in costs at differing levels relating to total dialings per phone hour, total decision-maker contacts per phone hour and total orders per phone hour. Such computations provide a realistic approach to determining breakeven point.

While these two worksheets relate to the sale of products or services, the same type of arithmetic can be structured to determine likely costs for literature requests, product information, customer service calls, sales support, full acount management, or sales promotion. The calls handled or made per hour might vary by application, but the principles are the same.

CALL RATIOS FAVOR TELEMARKETING

When comparing outbound sales calls to field sales calls the pure ratios favor Telemarketing. On the average, a field salesperson can make five to six calls a day—25 to 30 a week; on the average, a Telemarketing salesperson can make 25 to 30 decision-maker contacts a day (DMCs)—125 to 150 week.

Put another way, to achieve the same contact level, on average five field salespeople would have to be added for every Telemarketing salesperson.

SALES COST COMPARISONS

Using the sales call ratio advantage of Telemarketing as a base, let us now make sales cost comparisons, using a hypothetical case to illustrate the point.

The Case

A very successful industrial chemical company has built a multi-million-dollar business through the employment of a professional field sales staff. They have identified several SIC categories with prospects too numerous to cultivate. They wish to explore the potential of establishing an in-house Telemarketing sales staff whose charge will be to open new accounts in selected SIC categories.

The Starting Point

Knowing that management regards the present cost of acquiring new customers through a field sales force acceptable, the starting point is determining the present cost of acquiring new customers. And then following through to determine at what point the company recoups its original investment and reaches the breakeven point.

The Assumptions

For this hypothetical industrial chemical company, we will punch in the following assumptions:

1. The cost per field sales call has been computed at $180 each.
2. On the average, five field sales calls to bona fide prospects are necessary to acquire one new customer.
3. A total of three sales calls are made on each customer over a twelve-month period.
4. The average order written by the field sales force comes to $1,000.
5. The gross profit per order comes to $500.
6. For each 1,000 new customers acquired, 50% will order three times the first year; the other 50% will not repeat.
7. Of the 50% who become active customers the first year, 70% of those will remain active customers the second year, each reordering three times.

First-Year Results

Using the set of assumptions, let's now compute the investment on behalf of the field sales force in acquiring 1,000 new customers.

A. *Cost and Revenue Involving Acquisition of 1,000 New Customers*

	Cost		Revenue
5,000 field calls			
@ $180 each	$900,000	1,000 orders @ $1,000	$1,000,000
		Less Cost of Goods	500,000
		Gross Profit	$ 500,000
		Less Sales Cost	900,000
		Investment Total	($400,000)
		Investment per New	
		Customer	$ 400

Very simply, the company has an original investment of $400,000 for each 1,000 new customers acquired by the field sales force, or an investment of $400 for each new customer.

But the twelve-month cycle has just begun. According to the assumptions, two more calls will be made on each new customer before the first year of activity is completed. So let's take a look at where the company stands at the end of the first year.

B. *Cost and Revenue from Making Two Additional Follow-up Calls*

Cost		Revenue	
2,000 field calls			
@ $180 each	$360,000	Two additional orders @ $1,000 each from 500 customers	$1,000,000
		Less Cost of Goods	500,000
		Gross Profit	$ 500,000
		Less Sales Cost	360,000
		Profit on Repeat Business	$ 140,000
		Less Investment in New Accounts	400,000
		Investment First Year	($260,000)

There's improvement. The investment for each 1,000 new customers is down to $260,000, or $260 per customer. But we still haven't broken even. So we go into year two. Now the attrition rate drops off and 70% of remaining customers repeat three times during the second year.

C. *Year Two for Original Group of 1,000 Customers*

Cost		Revenue	
1,500 field calls			
@ $180 each	$270,000	Three additional orders @ $1,000 each from 350 customers	$1,050,000
		Less Cost of Goods	525,000
		Gross Profit	$ 525,000
		Less Sales Cost	270,000
		Profit on Repeat Bus.	$ 255,000
		Less First Year Investment	260,000
		End of Second Year	($ 5,000)

Obviously, two years is the magic period. For all practical purposes, the breakeven point comes early in the third year. And with a hard core of regular customers having been "paid for," substantial black ink can be expected by the end of the third year.

Having computed these figures the next logical step would be to use them as the norm for setting a goal for an in-house Telemarketing sales operation.

The Differences

In computing figures for an in-house Telemarketing sales operation, the major difference in cost involves the difference in number of calls per day by a field staff compared to an in-house Telemarketing staff. So if averages prevail, each member of the field staff would make five calls per day at a cost of $180 each. We'll assume each member of the Telemarketing staff will make thirty decision-maker contacts per day at a cost of $10.71 for each contact. (See "Computations" for "Basis for Expense Statement: Exhibit 10.2.")

Obviously, results by phone need not be anywhere near as productive because of the differences in selling costs. Difference would be as follows:

	Telemarketing	*Field Force*
Prospecting	5,000 DMC calls @ $10.71 ea.	5,000 calls @ $180
Repeat Business	3,500 calls @ $10.71 ea.	3,500 calls @ $180

Costs

Field Force	8,500 calls @ $180 =	$1,530,000
Telemarketing	8,500 DMC calls @ $10.71 =	$ 91,035
	Cost Difference	$1,438,965

Time Compression Potential

Building on our hypothetical case, let us now explore the time compression potential as it relates to acquiring 1,000 new customers. Our assumptions are as follows.

1. Our objective is to acquire 1,000 new customers.
2. On the average, five field sales calls are necessary to acquire one new customer.
3. Field sales personnel will make five calls a day.

4. Telemarketing sales personnel will make thirty decision-maker contacts a day.

5. Both the field sales representatives and the Telemarketing staff have a work year of 250 days (50 weeks × 5 days per week).

6. It is assumed that the field sales staff and the Telemarketing staff will be equally sales-efficient.

Field Sales Situation:

Some 1,000 man-days are needed to make 5,000 calls and thereby yield 1,000 new customers. If each representative makes five calls a day, it will take four field salespeople one year to complete the task.

Telemarketing Situation:

Using four sales specialists in a Telemarketing Center—sales efficiency being equal—making thirty decision-maker contacts a day, the same objective of 1,000 new customers will be reached in two months instead of twelve months. (And, of course, repeat business will materialize faster.)

The Question of Sales Efficiency

Our hypothetical case raises many questions:

1. Will the closure ratio of the telephone staff be the same as the field staff: one new customer, on average, for each five calls?

2. Will the first order come to $1,000 from phone solicitation?

3. Will 50% of telephone acquired customers buy twice more the first year?

4. Will 70% of the repeat customers from the first year repeat three times the second year at an average purchase of $1,000?

Only testing and time will provide the answers to these critical questions. But the favorable cost ratios of Telemarketing say clearly that the sales efficiency need not be anywhere near that of a field staff to result in a more favorable bottom line.

ATTACKING THE MARGINAL ACCOUNT PROBLEM

In the real sales world it is rarely a case of considering field sales *or* Telemarketing: more often than not it is a case of considering field sales *and* Telemarketing.

Most all sales organizations find that their customers break into three categories:

1. High-profit customers
2. Average-profit customers
3. Marginal-profit customers

It is in the marginal-profit customer category that the opportunity exists to change the numbers favorably for the entire sales organization. To explore this potential, let us structure another hypothetical case.

The Case

The ABC Company has a current list of 3,000 customers. One-third of their accounts are judged to be marginally profitable (i.e., this category does not result in the company's targeted profit of 15%). At present, sales calls made by the field force are scheduled as follows:

High-Profit Customers—twice a month

Average-Profit Customers—once a month

Marginal-Profit Customers—once every other month

Sales calls are estimated to cost $130 per call, well below the national figure of $205.40 per call.

Annual cost of sales calls—marginal accounts
    1,000 customers
    ×   6 calls per year
    = 6,000 calls @ $780,000 total cost

If Telemarketing Is Used

Now let us assume that we turn these marginal accounts over to a Telemarketing Center. And let us assume further that instead of a cost of $10.71 per decision-maker contact, we used in the previous hypothetical case, we apply a fully loaded cost of $20.00 per contact. Our numbers look like this.

    1,000 customers
    ×   6 calls per year
    = 6,000 calls @ $20 = $120,000 total cost
    Profit improvement—$660,000

Chances for Success

Since our Telemarketing contact costs are only 15.4% of those of the field force, chances for success are exceptional. And unlike our previous case that called for the Telemarketing Center to open new accounts without previous field force contact, here the Center would be servicing existing customers established by the field force. So the task of maintaining sales by phone would be simplified. Assuming equal productivity, this category of accounts would change from *marginal* to *high profit*, far exceeding the 15% profit goal.

But the advantages wouldn't end there for the Telemarketing Center would have freed the field force from 6,000 sales calls. This would open the door for more calls throughout the year to high-profit and average-profit customers, thus resulting in more sales and profits.

DEVELOPING A MEASUREMENT SYSTEM

We said at the outset of this chapter that Telemarketing should be measured on both a quantitative and qualitative basis. Quantifying sales is a simple matter, as we have seen. But qualifying factors should not be overlooked, such as more time available to call upon better customers.

Qualitative factors become major considerations when measuring the value of Telemarketing applications such as providing product information, solving customer, wholesaler and dealer problems, fulfilling literature requests, making Telemarketing a part of the sales promotion process and gathering market research data as part of the total Telemarketing process.

Chapter 2—"The GE Answer Center™"—shows the way to measuring qualitative factors. When Powell Taylor, manager of the center, was asked, "How do you know that the millions of dollars spent in building and maintaining the Center have been worth it?" he cited these measurement factors. "Surveys have shown that 95% of the callers to the center express satisfaction with the service."

Speaking of the impact of the program on dealers, Taylor cited surveys that showed that "more than 99% of surveyed dealers regard The GE Answer Center™ to be a 'super idea.'" These qualitative factors have convinced GE's top management that the program represents a competitive advantage for them.

An often-asked question is, "Is the cost of providing literature by phone request rather than by mail request justified?" How does one measure this? Surveys can give qualitative and quantitative answers: "Did you get the literature promptly?; Did you get our literature quicker than other literature you might have requested by mail?; Did our response prompt you to go to a dealer?; Did you buy?" Answers to such questions will provide qualitative and quantitative measurement, but with no basis of comparison.

To get comparative answers, controlled tests are indicated. To construct controlled tests, parallel markets should be selected. Market A advertising, for example, would offer literature by mail request only. Market B advertising would offer literature by either toll-free phone request or mail request.

Research would ask the same questions and make the same analysis for both markets. Such research would provide a measurement of (1) total literature requests from Market A versus Market B, (2) total cost per request from Market A versus Market B, and (3) total sales from Market A versus Market B. Most marketers who have tested phone requests against mail requests have found that phone requests come from more qualified prospects, resulting in more sales at the dealer level.

Another measuring device for Telemarketing applications is *market share*. We have only to go back to Chapter 5—"Telemarketing in the Sales Promotion Process"—to see how a major package goods company, Quaker Oats, built Telemarketing into their sales promotion and thereby increased market share dramatically. Used correctly, all Telemarketing applications have the potential of increasing market share.

Success is measured by the numbers. Telemarketing is measurable, quantifiable, and qualifiable. The numbers count.

CHAPTER II

Telemarketing in the Training Process

In Chapter 3— "The AT&T National Sales Center"—we were taken through the process of growth of a Telemarketing center from inception. And we learned what a major part motivation plays in sustaining success.

But all experts are in agreement: Success cannot be achieved or maintained without professional training. To get an insight to the training process, we traveled to the AT&T training center in Cincinnati, Ohio.

The man who heads up the training center is John R. Wood. His credentials are impressive. He started as a communications technician in 1968. From this launching point, he moved up the scale as technical instructor, operations supervisor, communications systems consultant, sales manager, national account manager, and staff manager. In 1981, he was promoted to Director–National Sales Center in Kansas City and in 1983 became Director of Sales and Marketing Education at AT&T Communications in Cincinnati.

A humble person, John Wood attributes a large measure of the success of the training center he heads to the professionalism of his staff. Two of his "heavy hitters" are Elaine Kaup, who is district manager–Sales and Marketing Education and Nancy Lamberton, staff manager.

TRAITS OF A TELEMARKETING PERSON

Our first questions were directed to Nancy Lamberton. We asked, "When recruiting, what traits do you look for?" She listed five traits.

1. Good communication skills—voice quality is clear and pleasant; articulate.
2. Persistent and able to bounce back from rejection.
3. Good organization skills.
4. Ability to project telephone personality—enthusiasm, friendliness.
5. Flexibility. Can adapt to different types of clients and new situations.

"We have potential applicants for Telemarketing sales positions go through a 1½ hour telephone assessment process," Nancy continued. "Applicants are put in several sales situations to determine if they have the dimensions we are looking for."

TRAINING FOR NEW HIRES

"Nancy, once a person is hired, what type of training program is that person put through?" She then proceeded to outline their training program covering a period of 18½ days.

1. Orientation (4 days)—Salesperson learns overall structure and goals of AT&T Communications as well as general business functions.
2. Network Services (2½ days)—Salesperson receives basic knowledge of AT&T Communications products and services. This is what the salesperson will be selling. This course is delivered via computer-based education.
3. Selling Skills (3½ days)—Salesperson learns sales skills through the interactive video disc, then goes through four hours of role plays with an instructor.
4. Telemarketing (2 days)—Salesperson learns how to identify client's needs and Telemarketing applications. Through casework, the salesperson practices implementing an application for a client.
5. Account Management (3 days)—Each salesperson has 400 accounts, which means that prioritizing accounts by revenue potential, cycling accounts, and time management are critical.

6. Advanced Account Management (3½ days)—After three to eight months of experience, the salesperson gets advanced training on how to manage the highest potential accounts.

THE SEVEN-STEP SELLING PROCESS

Students are schooled thoroughly in a seven-step selling process, a process developed over time, which leads the salesperson in logical steps from precall planning to the close and wrap-up. The outline that follows details these steps.

1. Precall Planning
   a. Reviewing client information
   b. Planning objective for the call.
   c. Psyching—getting mentally ready for the call!
2. Approach/Positioning
   a. Identify who you are and where you're from.
   b. Purpose of the call.
   c. Interest creating statement.
   d. Build rapport.
   e. Getting the decision maker.
   f. Getting through the receptionist/screener.
3. Data Gathering
   a. Gain general understanding of the client's business.
   b. Move from general to specific types of questions.
   c. Questioning techniques.
   d. Identifying a client business need.
4. Solution Generation
   a. Tailor communication solution to specific client need.
   b. Ask in-depth questions to test the feasibility of the solution.
   c. Gather data for cost/benefit analysis.
   d. Prepare client for the recommendation.
5. Solution Presentation
   a. Get client agreement to area of need.
   b. Present recommendation in a clear and concise manner.
   c. Use benefits.
6. Close
   a. Timing—when to close.
   b. Buying signals.

    c.   Handling objections.

    d.   Closing techniques.

7. Wrap-up

    a.   Implementation issues.

    b.   Thank client for the business.

    c.   Confirm client commitment.

    d.   Leave name and number.

    e.   Position next call.

APPLYING THE SEVEN-STEP SELLING PROCESS

Now let us see how this selling process might be applied outside of the field of communications. For our example, we'll create a wholesaler who specializes in veterinary drugs. The call is to introduce a new drug to a regular customer.

1. Precall Planning

The Telemarketer reviews the account file of the Whiteside Veterinary Clinic. He notes that Dr. Sargent ordered her usual order of drug supplies last month, but that she hasn't tried a new drug that L.L.M. Pharmaceutical has recently introduced via direct mail.

The Telemarketer reviews his introduction briefly, takes a deep breath, and says "Smile!"

2. Approach/Positioning

"Hello. This is Mark Wiley with L.L.M. Pharmaceutical. Dr. Sargent is usually available about this time. May I speak with her?"

"Good morning, Dr. Sargent. This is Mark Wiley with L.L.M. How have things been going at your clinic since I last talked to you? (Pause) I'm certainly glad to hear that! Dr. Sargent, as a buyer of many of our quality products, I knew you'd be interested in hearing about one of our innovative new drugs. If you have a minute, I'd like to ask you a couple of questions..."

3. Data Gathering

"Doctor, your practice pretty much covers a suburban area, doesn't it?"

"Right now when a dog is suffering from hookworm, what drug are you prescribing?"

4. Solution Generation

"Many vets also used to prescribe that particular drug. Have you had many dogs suffering from various side effects from that drug?"

"Would you be interested in prescribing a new drug that has few, if any, side effects?"

5. Solution Presentation

"L.L.M. has introduced Formula XYZ that not only has fewer side effects, but extensive laboratory tests have shown that the medicine takes effect twenty-four hours more quickly than similar drugs."

6. Close

"I'm sure that your customers would appreciate faster relief for their pets. Can I add a case of Formula XYZ to your regular order?"

7. Wrap-up

"I'm sure that you will be pleased with the results, Dr. Sargent. We've gotten excellent comments back from many vets around the country. I'll get that shipment to you by early next week. Thank you for your business. I'll be calling you again the first of next month. Have a good day!"

TEACHING OTHER SKILLS

"Successful telephone selling is the ultimate goal of our training," Nancy Lamberton said, "but sales success requires three additional skills: listening, making the prospect feel important, and time management.

"The ability to listen is uniquely important in Telemarketing," Nancy continued. "We do group roleplays where one student will build off the question of another student and the answer of the instructor who assumes the role of the prospect. What we try to do is to get a group of students to hold conversations with 'prospects' as if it were just one salesperson talking. This requires very good listening skills.

"We also have the students listen to an Abbott and Costello tape 'Who's on First.' When the tape is completed, the students have to identify the player's names. That requires active listening."

When it comes to making the prospect feel important, "It is essential that we teach telephone salespeople the importance of using the prospect's name in a natural way during the course of the conversation. And we stress active listening, plus focusing all of one's attention on the prospect," she said.

"Organizing time—time management—is a skill, a discipline that must be acquired if a Telemarketer is to experience a successful career path," Nancy continued. "Consequently time management is covered in several courses.

"One of our training techniques is to use an 'in-basket' exercise which demonstrates scheduling conflicts. We then teach the students how best to master scheduling. One of our teaching aids in this regard is Alan Lakin's excellent book *How to Control the Time of Your Life.*

"After the Telemarketer has been on the job for a while, a time log is kept to analyze patterns that develop. Corrective action is discussed, if necessary."

ROLE PLAYING: A KEY TEACHING DEVICE

"One of the most effective ways to teach proper Telemarketing procedures is to get students involved in role playing," Nancy Lamberton pointed out.

"Role playing is an excellent way to acclimate the student to the job," she said. "By putting students in different selling situations, we accelerate the learning curve. Students make their first mistakes with the instructor rather than the prospect."

Role Playing Examples

"Our instructors put students through role playing situations and then evaluate their performance," Nancy continued. We asked her to give us a poor example and a good example of a telephone dialogue with an evaluation for each. (These are abbreviated versions for demonstration purposes.) First we will give you the poor example.

HERITAGE VILLAGE FURNITURE
Poor Example

Sue: Hello. May I speak to Steve Rooney?
Steve: This is he.

Sue:	Oh, this is Steve? Well, Steve, this is Sue Jones, your new account executive. I'd like to talk to you about your phone services. Do you have a minute?
Steve:	I didn't catch the company you're with ...
Sue:	Oh, gosh, I'm sorry ... I'm with AT&T.
Steve:	Well, I'm pretty busy today ...
Sue:	That's okay, I won't take much of your time. Can I just ask you a few questions about your business?
Steve:	If it only takes a minute ...
Sue:	So, are you a furniture retail store?
Steve:	No, actually we manufacture furniture.
Sue:	Do you then sell it to retail furniture stores?
Steve:	Yes, we do.
Sue:	What is your sales volume a year?
Steve:	I don't see what business that is of yours. Anyhow, why are you asking me all these questions? What has it got to do with my phone service?
Sue:	Well, it helps me better understand your company so I can show you how to use Telemarketing.
Steve:	I'm not interested in Telemarketing. The way our business works, you can't sell furniture over the phone.
Sue:	A lot of companies are doing it.
Steve:	Well, not my company! Maybe you should call me back when you can tell me how to save on my phone bill. I'm really quite busy ...
Sue:	Can I call you tomorrow, Mr. Rooney?
Steve:	Why don't you just send something in the mail? That would be quicker.
Sue:	Oh, okay. I'll do that today. Thanks for your time, Mr. Rooney.

Now for the evaluation. (See Exhibit 11.1.)

ROLE PLAY/SKILL PRACTICE

Trainee: _Sue Jones_   Date: _6/16/84_

Which call (1st, 2nd, etc.) _2ND_   Case-Company name: _Heritage Village_

Instructor/Evaluator: _M. Pemberton_

Skill	Performance rating				COMMENTS
	ST	SAT	NI	NO	
APPROACH POSITIONING					Sue obviously didn't have a plan going into this call. She confused the client by not explaining who she represented and the purpose of the call. She also didn't get the client's attention.
Managed screener: polite, persistent, used as a resource				✓	
Completed positioning statement: who, where from, why calling			✓		
Made interest-creating opening statement			✓		The poor introduction set the tone of the entire call — Sue never recovered.
Asked for appropriate contact (if no name given prior to call)		✓			
Explained consultative role			✓		
Used listening skills		✓			
DATA GATHERING					Sue assumed Heritage was a retail store, which brought a negative response from the client. A series of close-ended questions then followed. Sue needs to ask more open-ended questions to get the client involved in the conversation.
Made appropriate transition from AP		✓			
Verified existing LD services				✓	
Asked about immediate concerns			✓		
Learned about business operations			✓		
Structured questioning strategy			✓		

Performance rating: ST – Strong; SAT – Satisfactory; NI – Needs improvement; NO – Not observed.

Exhibit 11.1.

184

Skill	ST	SAT	NI	NO	COMMENTS
Used open/closed questions appropriately			✓		*No strategy was poor. Before she got the client comfortable, Sue asked about sales/volume.*
Questions appeared directed toward objective(s)			✓		
Attempted to build credibility				✓	*At this point, the client's frustration with the call came out.*
Maintained conversational tone		✓			
Maintained control of dialogue			✓		
Demonstrated listening skills: -Probed and clarified -Paid attention to client -Followed client leads -Used silence -Demonstrated empathy -Tied together ideas			✓		
SOLUTION GENERATION/DEVELOPMENT					
Identified relevant/appropriate applications					
Collected appropriate specific data					
Dropped interest-creating hints					
Tailored application(s) to business operations & expressed needs					
SOLUTION PRESENTATION					
Reviewed & got agreement on client's objectives & concerns					
Tailored solution to client					
Focused on relevant benefits					
Demonstrated cost-effectiveness					
Anticipated impact of solution on client's business					

Exhibit 11.1, continued.

185

Skill	Performance rating	ST	SAT	NI	NO	COMMENTS
Made an organized presentation					✓	Sue tried to overcome the objection by talking about telemarketing. Many clients have preconceived notions about telemarketing. Don't throw the term around — show the client how it can benefit him!
Created interest and continuity in pres'n					✓	
Handled resistance & objections				✓		
Responded to buying signals					✓	
THE CLOSE						Sue let the client off the hook, which was probably a good choice considering how the call was going.
Timed the close right					✓	
Used appropriate technique(s)					✓	
Handled objections successfully					✓	
Gave client time to respond to close					✓	
Got clear commitment/Got an order					✓	
Wrapped up call: -Summarized call -Reinforced close -Arranged for next call -Clarified what client would do -Clarified what AE would do				✓		
FOLLOW-UP (if appropriate)						
Inquired about progress of implementation					✓	
Responded to client concerns					✓	

Exhibit 11.1, continued.

Let's deal with the same selling opportunity, but with a good example of how it might be handled.

HERITAGE VILLAGE FURNITURE

Good Example

Sue: Hello. This is Sue Jones with AT&T Communications. May I speak to Steve Rooney?

Steve: This is he.

Sue: Oh, good. How are you doing today, Mr. Rooney?

Steve: Well, actually I'm pretty busy today …

Sue: I understand that you're a busy person, Mr. Rooney, but if I can show you how to get the most out of your communication dollars would you have a few minutes to discuss some ideas?

Steve: Well, I guess I do have couple of minutes, but what can AT&T do for me?

Sue: As your account executive, I will be working with you to show you how AT&T long-distance services can be a valuable part of Heritage's profit picture. To see exactly how I can be of service to you, it would be helpful if I understood your business better. Tell me a little about Heritage Village Furniture, if you would …

Steve: We're a manufacturer of traditional home furnishings.

Sue: Who do you sell to, Mr. Rooney?

Steve: Various retail outlets such as local furniture stores. A lot of it is custom work, special orders.

Sue: Where are these outlets located?

Steve: Mostly in the eastern part of the country.

Sue: That's a large area. How do you reach all of your customers?

Steve: We have a sales force that visits the stores to keep our name in front of them. The salespeople show new samples of fabrics and promote sales we have going. The most important thing is that the furniture retailer remembers our name when his customer walks in the door.

Sue: Is that because you have a lot of competition?

Steve: You bet. I mean there are all sorts of furniture manufacturers. A lot of them with their own stores. We have to rely on the independent furniture store to sell our line.

Sue: Let's go back to your sales process. How do you get your orders?

Steve: Well, since most of the work is custom and we can never predict when an order will come in, most of the orders are mailed to us by the retailer. We have a form in the back of our sample book.

Sue: How long does it take to get that order in from the time it's mailed?

Steve: Oh, probably four days.

Sue: And how long does it take you to get the piece of furniture delivered to the customer once you've gotten the order?

Steve: Anywhere from six to eight weeks ... depends if we have all the materials in stock.

Sue: I remember when I ordered a chair recently, that sure seemed like a long time. Would you be interested in cutting down that delivery time?

Steve: Well, sure, but it takes that long to make the furniture—that can't be cut down.

Sue: Oh, I understand, Mr. Rooney. But perhaps we could cut down the time it takes you to get the order from the retailer. Would you be interested if I could show you a way to shorten those four days to just a few minutes to get that valuable order?

Steve: What do you have in mind?

Sue: Instead of using the mail for your orders, you could use
          a toll-free number for your retailers to call in their
          orders. Not only would you receive the order
          immediately, but you could also check on inventory
          while the retailer was on the line. If you were out of a
          fabric, say, the retailer could consult his customer to see
          what they wanted to do. This would save additional time
          and perhaps even the sale. Don't you think a toll-free
          number would give you a competitive edge?

Steve: Well, I don't know of anyone else doing that. But what
          kind of costs are we talking about?

Sue: I think you'll be surprised to see how inexpensive it is to
          provide this service to your customers. Our 800 toll-free
          number actually costs less than a regular long-distance
          phone call. So for a couple of dollars for the phone call,
          you'll be making a sale worth hundreds of dollars, plus
          improving your long-term relationship with the retailers.
          Can I place that order for you today?

Steve: How can I say no? Let's give it a try.

Sue: I'm sure you'll see immediate results. I'll give you a call
          in a few days to set the installation date. I really
          appreciate your business, Mr. Rooney. I look forward to
          working with you on this and perhaps other ideas.

Steve: Sounds good. Be talking to you soon.

Sue: Thanks again, Mr. Rooney. Goodbye.

Exhibit 11.2 reflects a much better evaluation than Exhibit 11.1.

ROLE PLAY/SKILL PRACTICE

ACCOUNT EXECUTIVE
TELEMARKETING SELLING SKILLS
Evaluation Sheets

Trainee: _Sue Jones_

Which call (1st, 2nd, etc.) _2nd_   Case—Company name: _Heritage Village_

Date: _6/16/84_

Instructor/Evaluator: _N. Tamburton_

Skill	Performance rating				COMMENTS
	ST	SAT	NI	NO	
APPROACH POSITIONING					Sue got the decision-maker to
Managed screener: polite, persistent, used as a resource				✓	talk to her by showing some empathy and creating some
Completed positioning statement: who, where from, why calling		✓			interest. This was very
Made interest-creating opening statement	✓				effective without being too pushy.
Asked for appropriate contact (if no name given prior to call)		✓			
Explained consultative role	✓				
Used listening skills	✓				
DATA GATHERING					Sue built her questions off the
Made appropriate transition from AP		✓			client's remarks, although she still kept the focus on her
Verified existing LD services				✓	objectives. Some more in-depth
Asked about immediate concerns		✓			questions may have been helpful, but Sue identified a business
Learned about business operations	✓				need.
Structured questioning strategy	✓				

Performance rating   ST - Strong; SAT - Satisfactory; NI - Needs improvement; NO - Not observed.

Exhibit 11.2.

Skill	Performance rating ST	SAT	NI	NO	COMMENTS
Made an organized presentation	✓				
Created interest and continuity in pres'n	✓				
Handled resistance & objections		✓			
Responded to buying signals		✓			
THE CLOSE					
Timed the close right	✓				Good timing and aggressiveness.
Used appropriate technique(s)	✓				Client's tone indicated that he
Handled objections successfully		✓			was interested, but he was
Gave client time to respond to close		✓			worried about cost. Sue overcame
Got clear commitment/Got an order	✓				the cost issue, and went for
Wrapped up call:					the close. Very effective!
-Summarized call					
-Reinforced close					
-Arranged for next call		✓			
-Clarified what client would do					
-Clarified what AE would do					
FOLLOW-UP (if appropriate)					
Inquired about progress of implementation				✓	
Responded to client concerns				✓	

Exhibit 11.2, continued.

191

Skill	Performance rating				COMMENTS
	ST	SAT	NI	NO	
Used open/closed questions appropriately		✓			
Questions appeared directed toward objective(s)	✓				
Attempted to build credibility		✓			
Maintained conversational tone	✓				
Maintained control of dialogue		✓			
Demonstrated listening skills: –Probed and clarified –Paid attention to client –Followed client leads –Used silence –Demonstrated empathy –Tied together ideas	✓				
SOLUTION GENERATION/DEVELOPMENT					
Identified relevant/appropriate applications	✓				
Collected appropriate specific data		✓			Overall, Sue did a good job. A few specific facts I like the value of a sale — would have helped build even a stronger case.
Dropped interest-creating hints		✓			
Tailored application(s) to business operations & expressed needs		✓			
SOLUTION PRESENTATION					
Reviewed & got agreement on client's objectives & concerns	✓				Sue used specific benefits to sell the client on the solution. Although she didn't use specific cost figures, her point was well made to the client.
Tailored solution to client		✓			
Focused on relevant benefits	✓				
Demonstrated cost-effectiveness		✓			
Anticipated impact of solution on client's business				✓	

MONITORING

"Role playing is a key teaching device in the initial training process," Nancy Lamberton said, "but it also serves a purpose in training seasoned Telemarketers in the introduction of new products and services. Continual monitoring by the sales manager is critical to the ongoing development of a Telemarketer," she added.

"With monitoring, not only can a manager provide feedback on areas that the Telemarketer needs to improve upon, but he provides motivation as well.

"A manager who monitors and gives constructive feedback on performance is viewed as being interested in the subordinate's growth and development. Typically, managers look at observable skills, skills such as following the seven-step selling process, product knowledge, enthusiasm, and listening skills."

AVAILABLE COURSES

Many of the courses at the AT&T Communications Planning Center are tailored specifically to AT&T needs, understandably. But the mission of the center includes providing basic training courses to personnel from other organizations. Elaine Kaup, District Manager, Sales and Marketing Education, told us there are two ongoing courses: one devoted to telephone selling skills, the other devoted to Telemarketing Center management. She provided us with the course descriptions, as contained in their literature, which follow on the next page.

The necessity of training is a given. From new hires to seasoned veterans, the process is never ending. Training the professional way is an investment in a healthy bottom line.

Telephone Selling Skills

Overview

This course is designed for sales and service representatives and managers responsible for selling or providing service by telephone. The three-day course examines various sales and service techniques in a Telemarketing center environment. Participants are introduced to various methods of increasing sales productivity and handling problem accounts.

Key Topics

- ☐ Communicating—Listening and Vocal Techniques
- ☐ Features vs. Benefits
- ☐ Preparation for the Call
- ☐ Call Handling Techniques, Fact Finding, Objection Handling and Close
- ☐ Role Play

Schedule

This course is offered once a month in Cincinnati and selected cities.

Telemarketing Center Management

Overview

Telemarketing is a concept that combines telecommunications technology, selling techniques, and management principles to create an integrated, disciplined system. This five-day, in-depth course is recommended for marketing managers of organizations dedicated to selling or providing service to customers via the telephone. Course content emphasizes the operational elements that must be considered when a large Telemarketing operation is established or modified. Casework and workshop activities provide opportunities for practical applications of the information presented.

Key Topics

- ☐ Center Strategy
- ☐ Promotion Management
- ☐ Human Resource Management
- ☐ Telemarketing Center Environment
- ☐ Communications and Information Management Systems

Schedule

This course is offered 8-10 times annually in Cincinnati and selected cities.

CHAPTER 12

Making the In-House/Service Organization Decision

When an organization decides to test Telemarketing they are faced with important decisions. Should we test Telemarketing in-house, or should we use a service organization? Or should we construct a dual test?: in-house and service organization. The wrong decisions can abort a marketing opportunity. Serious thought and careful investigation are imperative.

TYPES OF SERVICE ORGANIZATIONS

There are now over 200 service organizations performing Telemarketing services. But their expertise and services vary as much as the expertise and services of advertising agencies—from boutiques to full service.

Some service organizations simply take and transfer phone inquiries and orders: others create, perform and maintain complete Telemarketing programs. The former might best be described as *Telemarketing service bureaus;* the latter might best be described as *Telemarketing agencies.* Individual needs and capabilities dictate which type should be used if outside services are indicated.

DEGREES OF SERVICE

In structuring this important chapter, we had two options: (1) to survey scores of service organizations, simply tabulating the types of services they offer, or (2) to conduct in-depth interviews with a couple of highly regarded full-service Telemarketing agencies capturing the degrees of knowledge and service they are capable of delivering to the would-be Telemarketer. We opted for the latter based upon the theory that you want to know the maximum degree of help available from outside your organization.

Just one caveat: We are not saying that these are the only two outstanding full-service Telemarketing agencies—there are many. What we are saying is the two agencies we selected to help you in your decision-making process—in-house or outside service organization—are representative of the best.

PROS AND CONS

The first Telemarketing agency executive we interviewed was Jim McAllister, president of Telephone Marketing Services of Cincinnati, Ohio. Jim looks like and talks like an experienced sales and marketing executive. He is.

Jim McAllister discovered the practicality of Telemarketing for accomplishing marketing objectives while employed by the Market Development Department in the Tire Division of Uniroyal in the late 1960s. In early 1975, McAllister, with application and marketing knowledge gained over time, started Telephone Marketing Services. Today his organization performs full account management services for a wide variety of prestigious clients.

WHEN AN IN-HOUSE TELEMARKETING OPERATION IS INDICATED

The first question put to McAllister was a *zinger:* Under what conditions is it more appropriate for an organization to test and/or maintain a Telemarketing Center in-house? His answer was candid and precise:

"1. Situations which involve a great deal of technical knowledge.

2. Programs which require a high degree of integration with other internal support departments; close coordination of shipping schedules, inventories, credit, etc.

3. Programs which require a high degree of coordination with other departments; engineering for on-site field analysis, contract sales department, etc.

4. Order taking, public relations or educational contacts on a regular basis to a relatively small number of regular customers."

McAllister went even further. "Given the situation in which Telemarketing is used as an alternative to face-to-face contact and all other marketing factors remain constant," he said, "the following applications will prove difficult to impossible to accomplish even in-house."

- Capital expense items: high ticket, highly technical products
- Products or services requiring demonstration or on-site analysis
- Very complex selling situations involving committee decisions or multiple decision makers/influencers in large institutions

Just below these in degree of difficulty are situations involving:

- Fairly technical products to new accounts/markets
- New product to new market
- Multiple decision makers in smaller institutions

WHEN A SERVICE ORGANIZATION IS INDICATED

Jim McAllister then turned to situations in which, in his opinion, an outside service organization is indicated.

"1. Situations in which flexibility is required, such as several concurrent campaigns with varying objectives; seasonal selling programs or promotional campaigns.

2. Situations in which a full-time staff is either inadequate or cannot be justified, such as contacting a large universe over a short period of time; new product introductions; periods of exceptionally high incoming 800 number response; any short-term program.

3. Most sales support systems such as prospect qualification; lead generation; and new business or account campaigns.

4. Situations in which there is a lack of, or an unwillingness to commit internal resources such as quality management and personnel, administrative cost control, equipment, etc."

Speaking further on the inside versus outside issue McAllister observed, "When first considering Telemarketing, most companies initially turn to some form of outside assistance. This can range from various publications and seminars to training manuals and consultants. Many times this fact-finding process leads to the misconception that Telemarketing can provide spectacular results with very little effort and that it's relatively simple.

This perception not only creates unrealistic expectations, but often biases or prevents a thorough evaluation process that should include all the elements necessary for a successful program as well as all the factors which will create pitfalls and obstacles.

"The decision to do Telemarketing internally or through an outside supplier is often made prematurely," he said. "It should be determined *after* the evaluation process has led to the decision to test a specific program. The test phase definitely favors a good outside supplier. They have the organization in place, whereas the internal expertise, resources available and commitment at this stage are not normally sufficient to provide a valid test of potential.

"The decision to do Telemarketing inside or outside need not be a permanent 'either-or' decision," McAllister concluded, "since the variety and timing of Telemarketing applications can require outside support of in-house programs."

THE UNIROYAL EXPERIENCE

Having explored the parameters and the options for deciding to go inside, outside, or both, let us now explore applications that a professional Telemarketing agency of the caliber of Telephone Marketing Services might be able to execute. In the case of this agency, it all started with the Uniroyal experience.

The Uniroyal marketing department started by looking at segments of the tire market that required a considerable amount of service, but which were not favorable markets for sales. Car dealers were one of those segments.

The Uniroyal field force had to support the original equipment positions of car dealers. Dealers required a fair amount of service, taking up a lot of field sales' time, but they didn't buy many tires. The first step taken by the new Telemarketing Center was to combine sales effort and customer service, relieving the field staff of both efforts and releasing their energies for more profitable pursuits.

Then the Telemarketing Center started to package tires to the needs of car dealers rather than the needs of tire dealers. They changed offers to cater to this market segment. The new direction and the new selling and servicing method—Telemarketing—brought dramatic results. In less than two year's time, the car dealer segment went from virtually a minus category to $6 million plus.

Having hit pay dirt the first time out of the shoot, Uniroyal looked for applications in other divisions. The Keds Division proved to be an ideal candidate for Telemarketing applications.

Keds were sold by hundreds and hundreds of Ma and Pa footwear stores and by major department stores as well. The Ma and Pa stores moved considerable volume in the aggregate, but volume of individual stores when measured against cost of selling and servicing was less than exciting. The field force got their big volume and big commissions from selling the major department stores. The Telemarketing Center addressed themselves to both situations by selling and servicing Ma and Pa stores exclusively by telephone and performing a backup role for the salesperson in the case of major department stores.

A somewhat different role was performed on behalf of Uniroyal's Golf Division which they had at the time. Here they learned that a Telemarketing program worked very well for high-turnover, low-ticket items like golf balls and golf gloves. But when it came to clubs and bags a qualified lead generated by telephone, followed by a live presentation proved more sales efficient. When a customer became a full-line dealer, the Telemarketing Center handled all fill-in sales and service with the salesperson returning about once a year.

So Jim McAllister learned three valuable Telemarketing lessons while at Uniroyal, lessons that are applicable for both in-house and service supported marketing efforts:

1. Market segments that prove unprofitable for the field force can often be sold and serviced profitably by a Telemarketing Center.

2. Small dealers can often be better serviced and sold by a Telemarketing Center, leaving more time for the field force to sell major outlets.

3. Telemarketing can perform very well for the sale of high turnover, low ticket items, but the introduction and sale of major line items may best be left to the field sales staff who respond to telephone-qualified leads.

Having learned his lessons well, Jim McAllister launched Telephone Marketing Services. "With the blessing of Uniroyal," he stated proudly.

EXTENDING THE MARKETING PROGRAM

If his fledgling company was to succeed, McAllister decided, they must be capable of becoming an extension of the marketing department of any client they served. This meant his Telemarketing respresentatives had to know as much about any product line as the client's field force. And when new products or lines were introduced, the sales staff had to take and absorb the same training as the client's field force.

McAllister's firm was put to the test in early 1975 when they launched the Linde Division of Union Carbide, a division that sells welding equipment to plumbing and heating jobbers. (Union Carbide's direct sales force does not cover this trade.) McAllister's group became the sales force for the Linde Division. To serve in this capacity, Telephone Marketing Services took the following steps:

1. The assigned telephone sales staff went through a training program conducted by Linde personnel.

2. A list of targeted plumbing and heating jobbers was obtained from Linde along with all sales records of the customer base.

3. A dedicated phone number was established for the Linde Division so that all phone calls were answered with the client name.

4. In the test stage, all telephone communication was monitored by Linde personnel to make certain conversations reflected precisely the attitude and philosophy of the Linde Division.

5. All orders for welding equipment were transmitted to the factory daily.

6. Meticulous ledger records were maintained for each customer.

7. Sequence of follow-up calls to customers was scheduled based upon historic sales activity.

8. As new products and offers were developed by the Linde Division assigned telephone salespeople were indoctrinated by Linde personnel.

Did it work? The answer is that ten years after the first test McAllister's telephone sales staff was still performing as an extension of the marketing department of Union Carbide's Linde Division. So, surprisingly, it is possible for a professional Telemarketing agency to take on all the aspects of its client's sales force.

OTHER APPLICATIONS

We had more questions for Jim McAllister. In revealing the questions and answers we will, hopefully, be adding to your body of knowledge about Telemarketing.

Q. Is there any opportunity to sell package goods through Telemarketing?

A. Major department stores and the big chains tend to do their decision making at the headquarters level, often by committee. So Telemarketing doesn't fit the decision mode too well for these situations. But a major package goods category like coffee, for example, is also sold to nontraditional markets such as institutions. In those cases we can reach the decision maker by phone and perform very well.

Q. Jim, what would you consider to be the most overlooked application of Telemarketing in conjunction with a field force?

A. Servicing *open territories*, without a doubt. Selling being what it is, there is rarely a time for any sales organization when there isn't one or more open territory. Most firms just leave such territories unattended until they find a replacement, leaving themselves vulnerable to competition.

It's our experience that Telemarketing can fill the void very well in the interim. Customers really show empathy for the problem, a problem which many of them also face. And they truly appreciate the service and attention an experienced Telemarketing person can provide. Right next to open territories, I'd put *prospect qualification* as a much overlooked application.

Q. What is your reaction to some of the stigmas still attached to telephone selling—boiler-room activities, high-pressure selling, etc.?

A. First of all, every one of our programs is a dedicated program in that we are calling on behalf of our client. So the client name is actually being used. We perform as a separate Telemarketing division for the client. Therefore we convey whatever the company's selling philosophy is. Through product training, through client monitoring we take on the flavor of the company.

Q. Operating as you do—performing as an extension of your client's marketing department—how do you protect your client from a confidentiality standpoint?

A. In a manner very similar to a reputable advertising agency: (1) We will not handle more than one account in any business category without client permission; (2) we agree in writing not to divulge any confidential information; (3) we keep all records under lock and key.

Q. How do you select people to perform for your clients?

A. We look for pretty much the same type salesperson a client would hire as a field salesperson. We look for only full-time salespeople, people who respond well to training, people who thrive on challenges. The three most important characteristics we look for are *permanence, brains,* and *enthusiasm.*

Q. You are a strong advocate of testing, but tell us—what's the average duration of a test period?

A. A test period of six months is usually required to get definitive answers.

Thus ended a most informative and thought-provoking interview. Our next stop was New York City, where we interviewed another professional—Rudy Oetting, president of R. H. Oetting & Associates, Inc., whom you met previously in Chapter 10—The Mathematics of Telemarketing. Rudy Oetting specializes in telephone marketing management and sales and has worked with over 250 organizations dealing in consumer, industrial, institutional, and agricultural markets. He has shown them the way to achieve sales, produce leads, conduct surveys and provide customer services, both internally and through his affiliated agency, Telephone Marketing Resources, Inc.

Mr. Oetting has conducted Telemarketing seminars for the American Management Association and now conducts a series of Telemarketing management seminars for the Direct Marketing Association. He was generous in sharing seminar material with us.

TELEPHONE AS A MARKETING MEDIUM

Expounding on the growth of Telemarketing Rudy Oetting cited these comparative expenditure figures for 1982 versus 1983.

	1982 *(in billions)*	1983 *(in billions)*
Network cost	$12.5	$13.9
Labor cost	15.0	16.8(1)
Totals	$27.5	$30.7(2)
In-house expenditures	$27.2	$30.3
Agency/Service Bureau expenditures	$ .3	$ .4(3)

(1) Labor costs are going up at a slightly higher rate overall as more business-to-business operations come on stream.

(2) The total increase (11.6%) is higher than previous years with the now accelerated growth of all the operations added during the 1980–81 recession which are now reaping the benefit of the improved economy.

(3) There has been a dramatic increase in the number of agency/service bureaus which are becoming more regionalized in terms of clients and which are handling more business-to-business clients.

What these figures obviously disclose is that Telemarketing continues to grow and that the vast majority of such activity is performed in-house.

Referring to the potential of the telephone as a marketing medium, Mr. Oetting stated, "The telephone becomes a marketing medium when:

- People or organizations with an affinity for given products or services

- Are engaged by highly trained human beings

- In a controlled dialogue

- Supported by efficiently designed workflow, measurement and fulfillment systems

- Via telecommunications equipment and networks"

Citing the need to master the telephone as a marketing medium, Rudy Oetting presented a startling chart (Exhibit 12.1) that compares the rapidly descending cost of technology with the ever-increasing cost of labor, mail advertising, and travel expense. His projections indicate, for example, that the cost of communications equipment will drop over 40% in the 1990s over the 1980s. Contrast this with a projected 235% increase in labor costs and a 300% increase in travel expense. Those who master the power of Telemarketing will obviously enjoy a huge competitive advantage over those who don't.

"Not to be overlooked," Rudy Oetting said, "is the opportunity to deal with the negative impact of poor and indifferent customer service. People warn their friends against dealing with firms with whom they are dissatisfied," he said, "but rarely register their complaints with those who can rectify them. Telephone dialogues are the most effective way to uncover and rectify dissatisfaction," he concluded.

Rudy Oetting substantiated his stand by showing us the findings

TECHNOLOGICAL IMPACT ON COSTS
THE 1980'S DECADE—COST DYNAMICS

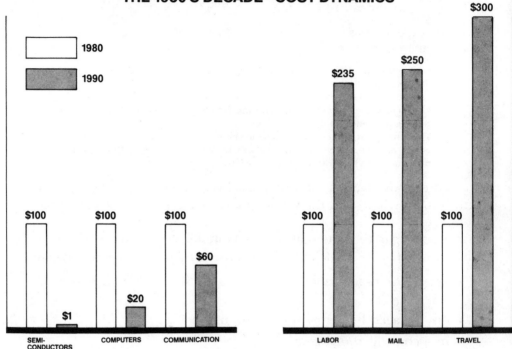

Exhibit 12.1.

reported in the February 1980 issue of *Small Business Reports* magazine that showed for every one complaint registered there are 50 unregistered complaints resulting in 550 warnings to friends and acquaintances. That can hurt. Bad!

ACHIEVABLE TELEMARKETING GOALS

Our final question to Rudy Oetting was, "What goals would you consider achievable for a firm you would consider to be a likely candidate for Telemarketing?" He listed six achievable goals.

1. Close sales
   - Sell
   - Take Orders
   - Upgrade Orders
2. Leads
   - Generate Leads
   - Screen and Qualify Leads

3. Gather Information
   * Surveys
   * Research
4. Provide Information
5. Improve Cash Flow
   * Credit checks
   * Collect Accounts
6. Customer Service

Our interviews with Jim McAllister and Rudy Oetting, we believe, are indicative of the help that is out there from competent professionals. And their input should go a long way toward deciding whether you should consider establishing an in-house Telemarketing Center, using a service organization, or doing both.

But should you decide to consider a service bureau, an agency, and/or consultant, there is one additional document you will want to have—a checklist.

SERVICE ORGANIZATION CHECKLIST

Depending upon your goals and needs, any number or all of the following questions are appropriate when interviewing a Telemarketing service organization.

18 Questions to Ask a Prospective Telemarketing Service Firm

1. Are your people full-time, or part-time?
2. What is the background of your principals?
3. What are your training procedures?
4. Will you allow us to put your assigned people through our product and sales training program?
5. May we monitor your test calls?
6. May we see your client list and may we call your clients to determine their satisfaction with your services?
7. Are you capable of surveying our marketing program and recommending Telemarketing applications? For whom have you done this?
8. Do you have any prior Telemarketing experience in our line of business?

9. If you recommend that we test Telemarketing, how many months do you believe it will take to get conclusive answers?

10. What is your ratio of supervisors to telephone communicators?

11. What is your incoming call capacity?

12. What is your outgoing call capacity?

13. How do you maintain inquiry/sales records for your clients?

14. How do you transfer information to your clients? By computer? Other methods?

15. Do you have any accounts at present that we might consider to be conflicts?

16. Would you agree not to take on any conflicting accounts as long as we are clients?

17. Would you agree to a confidentiality clause in our contract?

18. How do you charge for your services?

And so we come to the conclusion of "Successful Telemarketing." We have taken what we hope has been an interesting journey together, often exploring new and previously uncharted routes. In this journey we have all been privileged to meet people along the way whom we believe to be the smartest, the brightest, most experienced, most successful. Their generous contributions are beyond calculation.

In a world hungry for voice-to-voice attention, we have seen how Telemarketing has filled a communication void. In a selling arena beset by ever-spiraling costs, we have seen how Telemarketing can bring cost efficiency to one of the most honored professions.

The dramatic growth of Telemarketing is testimony to its universality: It is now a proven, professional approach to successful business practice. The applications apply to small businesses and large; to small customers and large; from simple products and services to complex, across industries, and in support of a variety of functions involving prospect and customer communication.

In summation, consideration of Telemarketing in the total marketing mix appears to be an imperative. The best of success to you!

Appendix

WORKSHEETS AND ANALYSIS FORMS

Note: The worksheets and analysis forms that follow are from a 152-page
manual—*The Telemarketing Edge: A Business Managers' Guide*—
copyright 1982, American Telephone and Telegraph Co.

Sales Activity/Profitability Analysis Worksheet

Salesperson: _____ Total Compensation (Salary & Expenses): _____

Account	Gross Sales	Cost of Goods	Gross Margin	Actual Number of Contacts	Selling Expenses	Net Profit	Net Profit Per Sales Call	Potential for Sales Increase
Total: _____				Total Number of Contacts: _____				

$$\frac{\text{Total Compensation}}{\text{Total Number of Contacts}} = \text{Average Cost Per Contact}$$

Average Cost Per Contact x Actual Number of Contacts = Selling Expenses.

Exhibit A.1. Sales Activity/Profitability Analysis.

Cost/Benefit Analysis
Objective:
Strategy:

	Telemarketing	Face-To-Face
Market Size:		
Contacts per customer per year		
Total Contacts Needed to Achieve Objective		
Contact to Objective Ratio*		
$ Value of Successful Contact		
Anticipated $ Benefit		
Number of Staff Needed		
Number of Supervisors		
Compensation		
Additional Expenses (e.g., T&E, incentive)		
Telecommunications and MIS Systems Costs		
Advertising and Promotion		
Overhead		
TOTAL COSTS:		

*Note: This can be sales/contact ratios or more complex ratios such as top prospects vs total inquirers. In that instance, $ value of successful contact would consist of sales conversion ratio applied to average sale.

Exhibit A.2. Cost/Benefit Analysis.

Customer Call Record

Name _____ Title _____

Name of business _____

Address _____

City _____ State _____ Zip _____

Telephone (area code) _____

Type of business _____

☐ Salesperson to visit

Date: _____ Time: _____ ☐ AM ☐ PM

☐ Literature to be sent

_____

Telemarketing Sales Specialist

_____

SEASONAL SALES SUMMARY	Jan	Feb	Mar	Apr	May	June	July	Aug	Sept	Oct	Nov	Dec
Product Ordered												
Amount of Order												
Customer Initiated												
Sales force initiated												

| Call Date | N.A. | Call Back | Call Details | Services/Products Sold | ADDITIONAL SALES | | | |
					Cross Sale	Upgrade Sale	Item	$ Value

Exhibit A.3. Customer Call Record.

Inquiry Response Record

Name   Title

Name of business

Address

City   State   Zip

Telephone (area code)

Type of business

Size of business   Credit rating

Comment

Nature of Inquiry

Prospect qualification

☐ **Incoming Call**   ☐ **Outgoing Call**

Date: Time: ☐ AM ☐ PM

☐ **Salesperson to visit**

Date: Time: ☐ AM ☐ PM

Telemarketing Specialist:

Total Time:

Call Date	N.A.	Call Back	Call Details	Services/Products Sold	ADDITIONAL SALES			
					Cross Sale	Upgrade Sale	Item	$ Value

Exhibit A.4. Inquiry Response Record.

Contact Narrative

Account Name		Tel. No.	
Date	Person Interviewed Services Discussed Changes	Quoted Order Number	Telemarketing Sales Specialist

Exhibit A.5. Contact Narrative.

Customer Service Call Log

Telemarketing Specialist: _____

Date/Time	Info Provided	Call Referred To	Comments

Exhibit A.6. Customer Service Call Log.

Telemarketing Sales Manager Log

Month of _____

Telemarketing Sales Specialists' Names	Total Number of Contact Attempts	Total Number of Sales Contacts	Total Number of Sales	Number of Contacts Per Sale	Gross Sales $	Gross Margin $	Total Sales Expense	Sales Expense Per Gross Margin $	Net Profit	Net Profit Per Contact
Department Totals										

Department Summary

Average Gross Sales per Contact: $\left[\dfrac{\text{Total Gross Sales}}{\text{Total Contacts}}\right]$

Cost per Sales Contact: $\left[\dfrac{\text{Total Sales Expense}}{\text{Total Contacts}}\right]$

Average Sales Expense per Gross Margin Dollar: $\left[\dfrac{\text{Total Sales Expense}}{\text{Total Gross Margin}}\right]$

Exhibit A.7. Telemarketing Sales Manager Log.

Breakeven Worksheet

Net Margin:

        Selling Price, per Unit_____

(less)   Cost of Goods Sold, per Unit_____

    = Gross Margin/Unit_____

(less)   Order Processing, Shipping,
        Handling, Warehousing, Other
        Attributable per Unit Costs_____

    = Net Margin/Unit_____

Promotion Expenses:

        Cost of Production_____

(plus) Cost of Mail/Advertising_____

    = Total Promotional Costs $_____

Breakeven:

        Total Promotion Expenses_____

        Divided by Net Margin Per Unit_____

    = Number of Unit Sales Needed
        to Break Even_____

To calculate response % needed, divide number of unit sales by total number on mail list and/or target market advertising circulation.

Exhibit A.8. Breakeven Worksheet.

Creative Input Brief: Development of Promotions and/or Sales Strategy

(Note: all organizations involved in the Project should complete this brief and submit to Project Leader for Review. A Single Input Brief reflecting the consensus of opinion should be prepared by the Project Leader and signed-off by each involved organization.)

Date:

Product/service description:

If service, products involved:

Target audience:

Primary Benefits:	Related product/feature:
1.	1.
2.	2.
3.	3.

Secondary Benefits: (not necessarily mentioned in program)	
1.	1.
2.	2.
3.	3.

Competition to the product/service, if any:

Offer (what is it?):

What elements should be tested in this mailing?

Specifics to be stressed:
1.
2.
3.

Specifics to be avoided:
1.
2.
3.

Fullfillment needs:

Exhibit A.9. Creative Input Brief.

GUIDELINES FOR TELEPHONE MARKETING PRACTICES*

PROMPT DISCLOSURE
Article 1

All telephone marketing contacts should promptly disclose the name of the sponsor and the primary purpose(s) of the contact. No one should make offers or solicitations in the guise of research or a survey when the real intent is to sell products or services, or to raise funds.

HONESTY
Article 2

All offers should be clear, honest and complete so that the recipient of the call will know the exact nature of what is being offered and the commitment involved in the placing of an order. Before making an offer, direct marketers should be prepared to substantiate any claims or offers made. Advertisements or specific claims which are untrue, misleading, deceptive, fraudulent, or unjustly disparaging of competitors should not be used. All documents confirming the transactions should contain the means for the customer to contact the telephone marketer.

TERMS
Article 3

Prior to commitments by customers, all telephone marketers should disclose the cost of the merchandise or service, all terms, conditions, payment plans and the amount or existence of any extra charges such as shipping and handling.

REASONABLE HOURS
Article 4

Telephone marketers should avoid making contacts during hours which are unreasonable to the recipients of the calls.

USE OF AUTOMATIC EQUIPMENT
Article 5

No telephone marketer should solicit sales using automatic dialing equipment unless the telephone immediately releases the line when the called party disconnects.

Telephone marketers should avoid using such devices as automatic dialers and pre-recorded messages when in violation of tariffs, state or local laws, or these Guidelines.

*Direct Marketing Association, Inc., 6 East 43rd Street, New York, NY 10017.

TAPING OF CONVERSATIONS
Article 6

Taping of telephone conversations should be conducted only with all-party consent or the use of a beeping device.

NAME REMOVAL
Article 7

Telephone marketers should remove the name of any contact from their telephone lists when requested to do so.

When possible, telephone marketers should offer to remove consumers' names from lists that are offered to other telephone marketers.

MINORS
Article 8

Because minors are generally less experienced in their rights as consumers, telephone marketers should be especially sensitive to the obligations and responsibilities involved when dealing with them.

PROMPT DELIVERY
Article 9

Telephone marketers should abide by the FTC's Mail Order Merchandise (30-day) Rule when shipping prepaid merchandise.

As a normal business procedure, telephone marketers are urged to ship all orders as soon as practical.

COOLING-OFF PERIOD
Article 10

Telephone marketers should honor cancellation requests which originate within three days of sales agreements.

RESTRICTED CONTACTS
Article 11

Telephone Marketers should avoid calling telephone subscribers who have unlisted or unpublished telephone numbers unless a prior relationship exists.

LAWS, CODES AND REGULATIONS
Article 12

Telephone marketers should operate in accordance with the laws and regulations of the United States Postal Service, the Federal Communications Commission, the Federal Trade Commission, the Federal Reserve Board and other applicable Federal, state and local laws governing advertising, marketing practices and the transaction of business by mail, telephone, and the print and broadcast media.

MAJOR COMPANIES THAT PRACTICE TELEMARKETING

	Order Processing	Customer Service	Field Sales Support	Account Management
ADP			X	
ADT			X	
Aetna Life & Casualty			X	X
Air Products & Chemicals	X	X	X	
Alcoa	X	X	X	
American Airlines	X	X	X	X
American Can Co.	X	X	X	
American Cyanamid	X	X	X	X
American Express	X	X	X	X
AMFAC, Inc.	X			
Arco	X	X	X	
Ashland Oil		X		
Associated Dry Goods	X			
Bache Group	X	X	X	X
Beatrice Foods	X	X		
B. F. Goodrich	X	X	X	X
Boise Cascade	X	X	X	
Borden	X	X		
Bristol Meyers	X	X	X	
Burroughs		X		
CBS	X	X	X	X
Champion International	X	X	X	X
Chrysler Corp.	X	X	X	X
Colgate Palmolive	X	X	X	X
Conrail	X	X		
Consolidated Freight	X	X	X	X
Continental Airlines	X			
Continental Grain		X	X	X
Corning Glass Works	X	X	X	
Dean Witter Reynolds		X	X	
Deere & Co.			X	
Delta Airlines	X			
Digital Equipment Co.	X	X	X	X
Dow Jones		X		
Dresser Industries	X	X	X	
Eastern Airlines	X			
Eastman Kodak		X	X	X
E. F. Hutton			X	
E. I. Dupont	X	X	X	X
Electronic Data Systems	X	X		

	Order Processing	Customer Service	Field Sales Support	Account Management
Exxon	X	X	X	X
Firestone Tire	X	X	X	X
Ford Motor Co.	X	X		X
Geico	X	X	X	X
General Electric		X		
General Motors		X		
General Tire	X	X		
Georgia Pacific	X	X	X	
Harris Equipment	X	X	X	
Hercules	X	X	X	X
Hewlett Packard	X	X	X	X
Honeywell Inc.		X	X	
Hilton, Inc.	X			
Holiday Inns	X			X
Howard Johnson	X	X	X	
Humana Inc.			X	X
Hyatt	X			
IBM	X	X	X	
INA		X	X	X
Ingersoll-Rand	X	X		
International Harvester	X	X	X	
International Paper	X	X	X	X
ITT	X	X		
J. C. Penny	X	X		
John Hancock Mutual	X	X		
Johnson & Johnson	X			
J. Ray McDermott	X	X	X	
3M Corp.	X	X	X	X
Martin Marietta	X	X	X	X
Marriot Corp.	X			
McGraw Hill	X	X	X	
Merrill Lynch		X	X	
Monsanto	X	X	X	X
Montgomery Ward	X	X		X
Mobil Oil	X			
Mutual of Omaha		X	X	
Nabisco	X		X	
National Data	X			X
Nationwide Group			X	
NCR	X			
Norton Simon	X		X	
Owens-Illinois	X	X	X	X

	Order Processing	Customer Service	Field Sales Support	Account Management
Pan Am	X			
Pennwalt	X	X	X	X
Pepsico	X		X	X
Phillip Morris	X		X	X
Phillips Petroleum		X	X	
Polaroid	X	X		
P.P.G. Industries, Inc.	X	X	X	
Prudential		X	X	X
Quality Inns	X			
Ralston Purina		X	X	X
Ramada Inn	X	X		
Republic Airlines	X	X		X
Rohm & Haas	X			
Ryder System	X	X	X	X
Sears Roebuck	X			
Schering Plough				X
Sheraton	X			
Sherwin Williams	X	X	X	
Sperry Rand			X	
Standard Oil	X	X		
Sun Company, Inc.	X	X	X	X
Teledyne		X		X
Tenneco	X	X	X	X
Texas Instruments	X	X	X	
Textron			X	
Time, Inc.	X	X		X
Transamerica Corp.	X	X	X	X
Transworld Corp.	X			X
Travelers Corp.		X	X	
U. S. Steel	X	X	X	X
Union Carbide	X			
Union Oil of LA	X		X	X
United Airlines	X			
United Parcel Service	X	X		
Warner-Lambert	X	X	X	X
Western Airlines		X	X	
Western Electric	X			
Westinghouse Electric			X	
Westin Hotels	X			
Weyerhauser	X	X	X	X

Telemarketing
Glossary of Terms

Abandoned Calls —Calls answered by equipment in a Telemarketing Center, but that never reached a telephone specialist because the caller hung up, usually due to a long wait.

Account Executive —Salesperson who performs sales and service responsibilities for their assigned accounts via Telemarketing.

Account Management —Telemarketing application in which Telemarketing specialists replace an outside sales force by initiating and completing all sales transactions for various types of accounts via the telephone.

Account Pairing —Pairing specific office staff members, trained in Telemarketing with specific field sales people to share full sales responsibility for their assigned accounts.

Accuracy —Degree of similarity between the characteristics of an audience that receives a promotional message and the characteristics of the target market group of customers.

After Call Work Time —Time required by a telephone specialist after a call to complete the record of that call and to arrange for fulfillment implementation.

After Market —Markets that develop for the accessories or parts of a product after the product's initial sale (e.g., paper or toner sales to a copier purchaser).

AT&T 800 Service —Inward WATS service allowing callers to call without charge or operator intervention. The call recipient pays for the call.

AT&T Advanced 800 Service —Additional service features that allow business customers to be more flexible and responsive in managing their toll-free calling networks.

AT&T 800 Single Number Service —Permits the customer to advertise one AT&T 800 service number for access to multiple interstate and intrastate locations and to multiple groups of lines at the same location.

AT&T Customized Call Routing —Permits the customer to specifiy the terminating points for calls originating from selected geographic areas.

AT&T 800 Time Manager —Allows calls to be routed differently depending on the time of day. A day is defined as midnight to midnight. This feature assumes a repeating 24-hour cycle. Time intervals are specified on the quarter hour.

AT&T 800 Day Manager —Allows calls to be routed differently depending on the day of the week. A week is defined as Sunday through Saturday.

AT&T 800 Call Allocator —Allows subscribers to apportion calls to two or more call-answering locations by determining the percentage of calls each location should receive.

AT&T 800 Call Prompter —Allows the caller to hear a recorded message which requests that they dial additional digits in order to route their call to the department or service of their choice.

AT&T 800 Command Routing —Allows subscribers to respond to spontaneous needs such as emergencies, by establishing alternate ways for AT&T 800 Service calls to be routed. On command from the subscriber, calls would be switched to preplanned alternate routes.

AT&T 800 Routing Control Service —Permits the subscriber to change their AT&T 800 Routing Service routing plan on a real-time basis from a CRT located on their premises.

AT&T Call Attempt Profile —This feature provides data samples reflecting attempted calls to a given 800 number. The report provides a summary of the number of call attempts to an 800 number by the area codes from which the calls originated, by the time of day and by the date the call originated, depending on the specified day(s) a customer wishes to study.

AT&T 800 Service-Canada —A network that allows a customer in the contiguous United States to subscribe to dedicated access lines in order to receive calls from a subscriber service area composed only of Canadian area codes.

AT&T Long Distance Service —Common term for AT&T MTS—Message Telecommunications Service.

AT&T WATS Service —Long-distance service for outgoing calls to specific service areas both in-state and out-of-state at a lower cost than AT&T Long Distance for large calling volumes.

Automatic Answering Machine —Plays and records messages when the called party is unavailable.

Automatic Call Distribution Systems (ACD) —Incorporates both functional and informational advantages for Telemarketing Center managers, such as automatic and equitable distribution of incoming calls, and queuing of calls. It also provides real time management information to determine the number of specialists and network service lines necessary for the center to function efficiently and effectively.

Automatic Computer Record Dialing Machine —Machine that dials a preprogrammed telephone number, and plays an automatic recording, normally a sales pitch.

Automatic Dialers —Telephone feature or stand-alone device that stores telephone numbers in memory for future access and automatic dialing.

Average Speed of Answer —Average length of time it took for all agents to answer all calls during a measured period.

Average Talk Time —Average length of time all agents talked on all calls during a measured period.

Benefit Selling —Selling based on conveying to the prospect how a product's capabilities will meet his particular needs.

Blocked Calls —Calls that are not completed because a customer receives a busy signal.

Boiler Room —Telephone selling that lacks professionalism due to concentration on call volume and high pressure.

Burnout —Marked deterioration in performance or motivation of a Telemarketing representative. A condition generally due to an excessively long period of time on the telephone with no opportunity for other tasks.

Business-to-Business Telemarketing —Marketing to businesses, usually segmented by industry, function, or job title.

Business-to-Consumer Telemarketing —Marketing to individual people at their residences.

Call Management —Process of selecting, based on detailed information of telephone activity and costs, the optimum mix of terminal equipment, network services, and staffing to achieve maximum productivity and service from a Telemarketing Center.

Call Sequencer —Stand-alone device that generally provides call distribution to telephone specialists, queuing, and recorded announcement for callers. A device similar to an ACD, but with less features.

Caller Personalties —Describes a person who has the ability to establish a personal relationship via the telephone and not be merely a voice.

Close-Ended Questions —Used to elicit a specific, usually one-word, response.

Cold Calls —Sales calls to prospects.

Computer Response Time —Time elapsed between a telephone request for information from a terminal and when that information is received by the terminal, available for the agent's use on a call.

Consultative Selling —Highly personalized sales process that identifies customers particular needs and then sells products or services to meet those needs.

Cost/Benefit Analysis —Identification and evaluation of the expenses and opportunity costs versus the possible revenue and profit streams associated with purchasing a product or service.

CPI —Cost per inquiry.

CRT (Cathode Ray Tube) —The viewing screen of a computer terminal.

Cross-Selling —Selling an additional product or service—usually related—to a customer.

Customer Cycling —Planned periodic recontacting of a customer.

Customer Profile —Contains buying history, payment record, and financial, demographic, industry and job title information of the potential buyers of a product or service.

Customer Service —Provides, usually in response to a customer-initiated call, services such as locations of retail dealer, product information, complaint handling, order status, service information, or emergency response.

Customer Service Representative —Person working in a computer-based operation that links service and information with production, planning and credit functions of an organization.

Database —Collection of facts used to support the information requirements in order to perform a specific task or function. The term is generally used in reference to an automated system.

Data Processing —Manual or computerized manipulation of data to determine specific information. Functions may include recording, classifying, sorting, summarizing, calculating, disseminating or storing data.

Demographics —Personal and social-economic information or statistics about an individual or group that may provide insight to their life style or values.

DIAL-IT* 900 Service —Telecommunications service that can be utilized as a polling service or as a way of delivering a recorded or live message. The costs of the call are paid by the caller.

Direct Inward Dialing —Allows a person to receive a telephone call without going through an incoming operator or switchboard.

Direct Marketing —Total of activity by which the seller effects the transfer of goods and services to the buyer, directs its efforts to a qualified audience, using one or more media to solicit a response from a prospect or customer.

*Service Mark of AT&T

Direct Response —Action taken as a result of receiving an advertising message via any medium.

Electronic Mail —Process of sending messages electronically from a computer terminal to another terminal.

Electronic Marketing —Method of conducting sales functions and assisting customers that utilizes a whole host of sophisticated media, data communications, and telecommunications support elements.

Ergonomics —Science that studies the problems of people adjusting to their environment and subsequently seeks to adapt working conditions to human limitations.

Experience Curve (also known as a learning curve) —As people gain more experience in a given situation, their efficiency and effectiveness are optimized.

Follow-up System —System that determines current status on leads that have been passed on or schedules future customer contacts.

Guided Scripting —May use scripts for key sections, but generally uses key words or prompters to allow the telephone representative to personalize the call, resulting in a more natural, effective contact.

High Volume Accounts —Customer accounts with a large number of transactions per period as compared to other accounts.

Hotline —Customer service application that allows a customer to call a specified number to express their concerns or to seek information.

Inbound —Calls that are received at a Telemarketing Center.

In-House Telemarketing —Telemarketing operations being performed by specially trained internal personnel of a company to market and sell that company's own products.

Inside Sales —Telephone sales as opposed to field sales.

Interpersonal Communications Skills —Ability to listen, to establish rapport and to present self and ideas clearly and concisely. In Telemarketing, this must be done with voice and manner control.

Junk Phone Calls —Unwanted, cold sales calls, primarily those received at residences, that are the Telemarketing equivalent to junk mail due to lack of target marketing.

Lead —Potential customer who has inquired or indicated interest.

Leadflow —Volume of leads over time.

Lead Generation —Stimulation through the use of any medium.

Lead Short Falls —Insufficient quantity or quality of leads generated by a media stimulus.

Lead Swamping —Generation of more leads than can be followed up or qualified by a sales force in a timely fashion.

Lead Qualification (also referred to as prospect qualification) —Interaction with potential customers to determine the level of interest and the willingness and ability to buy a specific product or service.

Leadflow History —Historical record of leads generated by different offers in different media or from different sources.

Leadflow Management —Qualification of leads in order to assure that each inquiry receives an appropriate and timely response. Also refers to timing of stimuli to generate a response rate that may be effectively answered.

Leadflow Monitoring —Tracking of leads by media and/or ad copy and design; also, rate of lead response measured against ability to qualify or respond to the lead.

Leadflow Planning —Strategy to determine and control the flow of responses to a planned stimulus.

Loose Leads —Leads generated as a result of giving a modicum of information about a given proposition with an attractive reward for responding.

MIS (Management Information System) —Systems that supply sales support information which the specialist needs to perform a function and that supplies the information which management needs to manage and evaluate performance.

Marginal Account —Accounts whose low volume of sales or remote geographic location make the use of a field sales force low in productivity and high in cost.

Market Test —Trial introduction of a new product to an existing market or of an existing product to a new market.

Marketing Communications Mix —Selection and integration of various means that businesses use to communicate and market to their customers, such as advertising, trade shows, field sales force, and Telemarketing.

Marketing Mix —Interrelated marketing elements—product, price, place and promotion—that must be "blended" together to achieve a combination that will produce profitable sales.

Marketing Strategy —Fundamental marketing logic by which the business unit intends to achieve its marketing objectives. Marketing strategy consists of a coordinated set of decisions on target markets, marketing mix, and marketing expenditure level.

Maximum Delay —Longest time a caller was held in queue waiting for a telephone specialist during the measured period.

Monitoring —Listening to and evaluating a telephone call in order to develop the telephone specialist's skills.

On-Line —Real-time connection to a computer.

Open-Ended Question —Normally prevents specific yes/no answers, thereby requiring the respondents to reply in their own words.

Open Territories —Areas not assigned to a field sales force.

Order Processing —Telemarketing application that at the most basic level consists of simply recording and processing orders phoned in by customers. Slightly more complex applications include cross or upgrade selling, seasonal selling, renewals, catalog selling, and reservations as part of the order entry activity.

Orphan Accounts —Accounts not currently being served by a sales representative.

Outbound —Calls made to a prospect or customer from a Telemarketing Center.

Pilot —Trial program designed to measure the potential of a Telemarketing application.

Pre-Call Planning —Preparation and activity that is required in advance of a sales call for a telephone specialist to have an effective call.

Private Branch Exchange PBX —On-premise switching system that allows communication within the business and between the business and the outside world.

Product Information —Specific application for a Telemarketing Center which provides customers with information on various products or services.

Program Management —Monitoring the development of a program from its inception to its conclusion.

Projected Response —Volume and rate response anticipated based upon historical data to a given stimulus.

Promotion Management —Telemarketing application that uses innovative promotion techniques capable of generating rapid customer response via advanced telecommunications technologies.

Prospect Profile —Delineation of all known descriptors of the potential buyers of a product or service, includes financial, demographic, industry, and job title information.

Psychographics —Life styles and attitudinal characteristics used to refine and target a marketing program.

Qualified Leads —Potential customer who has met defined criteria for acquiring a product or service.

Queue —Stacking of calls in an ACD, with the oldest call in line handled first.

Remote Call Forwarding (RCF) —Local telephone number in a distant city that, when called, automatically routes to your location without the caller being aware of the process. The call recipient pays for the call.

Roll-Out —Phased implementation of an entire Telemarketing program after evaluating the results of a pilot.

Sales Conversion Rate —Number of sales made in comparison to the number of inquiries or calls initiated.

Sales Support —Telemarketing application that provides the field sales force with an "inside" contact who performs a variety of support functions such as qualifying leads, performing credit or inventory checks, tracking orders and shipments, or entering orders.

Script —Prepared text presentation that is closely followed by Telemarketing specialists as a tool to convey a specific sales message to the customer.

Speed Dial —Telephone feature that allows frequently dialed numbers to be programmed and stored for one button dialing.

Telecommunications —Electronic transmission of audio or data information.

Telemarketer —Also known as specialist, representative, agent; generally a person who makes or takes calls as part of a Telemarketing operation. (See also Account Executive and Customer Service Representative.)

Telemarketing —Telemarketing is a new marketing discipline that utilizes telecommunications technology as part of a well-planned, organized, and managed marketing program that prominently features the use of personal selling, using non-face-to-face contacts.

Telemarketing Agencies —Create, perform, and maintain complete Telemarketing programs.

Terminals —Generally a Cathode Ray Tube (CRT) with keyboard that allows access to an information database or the ability to input information to a database.

Test Market —Discrete trial market for a new product, customer group, or offer.

Tight Leads —Leads generated as a result of giving a great deal of information about a given proposition with little or no reward for responding.

Toll Free 800 Service —Inward WATS service allowing callers to call without charge or operator intervention. The call recipient pays for the call.

Trunk Capacity —Number of outgoing or incoming circuits connecting your site to the telephone company.

Index

233